Part 1

What is Tripe?

According to the Oxford English Dictionary, the word tripe comes from the Old French "Tripe" or "Trippe", meaning the entrails of an animal, and the principal meaning is the first or second stomach of a ruminant, especially of the ox, prepared as food. (Formerly the word could also refer to the entrails of swine or fish.)

An ox's stomach is very large, occupying threequarters of the abdominal cavity. It consists of four parts; the rumen, reticulum, omasum and abomasum, the last named having a mucous membrane and popularly termed the "true" stomach.

An ox weighing between 700 and 800 pounds will produce about 15 pounds of tripe, although tripes can vary from 14 to 30 pounds in weight, depending on the age and breed of the animal. The rumen, or paunch, is the largest part of the tripe, and is known as "seam". The walls of the reticulum, or second stomach, are covered with branched ridges, giving it a honeycomb appearance, which gives this part its name. "Leaf" tripe is so called because of the membrane of leaf-like folds of the abomasum; this has a high fat content. Another part of the animal, the oesophagus or food pipe, is also classed as tripe, and is known as "weasand". All these parts pass

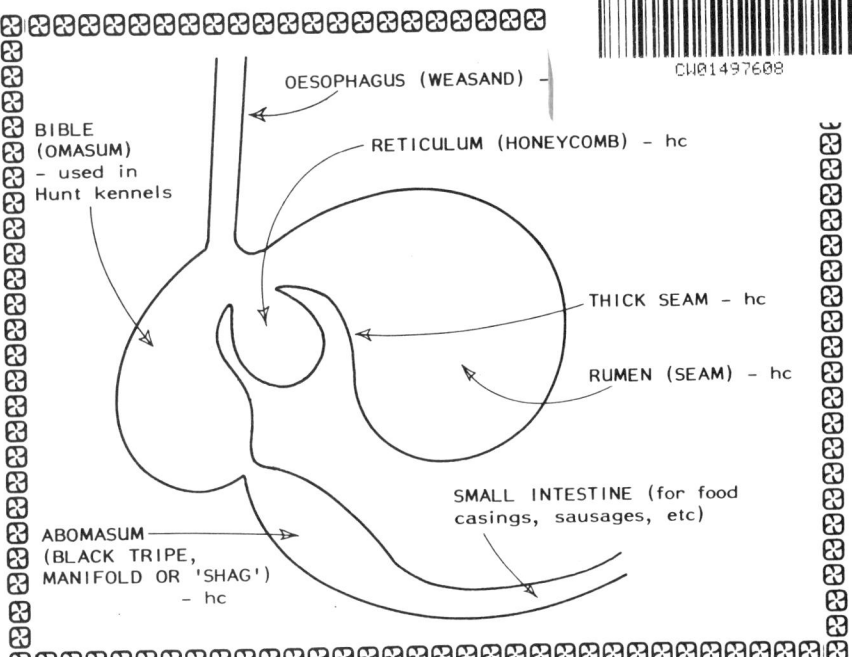

through the same cleaning and preparation processes.

Tripes from other animals are also considered edible. Sheep's tripes, for example, are used in the preparation of "Pieds Paquets a la Marseillaise" and "Petarram", two delicacies of South West France. The use of the first stomach of beef is well known in dishes such as the famous "Tripe a la mode de Caen" and "Gras-double a la Lyonnaise", another French speciality. Finally, of course, the intestines of pigs have long been used to enclose sausages.

Early History

The origins of tripe dressing are lost in the mists of time. It has a known history of over 2,000 years, having been esteemed by both the Greeks and the Romans. Athenaeus praised it; Homer, the Father of Greek poetry, noted the excellence of the tripe prepared in honour of Achilles; Mouffet and Bennett (1655) declared that: "The taste of Tripes did seem so delicate to the Romans, that they often killed oxen for the Tripes' sake."

It was said that William the Conqueror enjoyed tripe accompanied by Neustrian apple juice. However, it is unlikely that the cooks of the Middle Ages were adept in the preparation of tasty, well-seasoned dishes!

The Oxford English Dictionary cites numerous early references to tripe. It is mentioned by Langland in "Piers Ploughman", by Caxton and, of course, by Shakespeare, whose character Grumio enquires, in "The Taming of the Shrew", "How say you to a fat tripe - finely broiled?" In 1541 Sir Thomas Elyot gave a description of "the inwards of beastes, as trypes and chytterlynges." (Chitterlings are the smaller intestines of the beast, prepared for eating by frying or boiling.)

In 1662 Samuel Pepys wrote: "Dined with my wife upon a most excellent dish of tripe of my own directing - covered with mustard - of which I made a great meal." A year or so later he again records: "Home to dinner on tripes."

Raw tripes before processing

Arbuthnot's "Harmony in Uproar" begs "To invite you to eat a Tripe-soup and Fricassey of Sheep's Trotters." Oliver Goldsmith praised the dish, as did Charles Dickens. In "Barnaby Rudge", one of the characters was regaled with "A steaming supper of boiled tripe and onions, to which meal he did ample justice." It has been said that King Edward VII was also fond of a dish of tripe.

The word "tripe" was sometimes used in a derogatory sense, when applied to a person. "Tripe-cheeks", for example, described someone with coarse, blowsy cheeks. Shakespeare, in "Henry V", wrote: "Thou damned Tripe-visag'd Rascall."

A "Tripe-wife" was a female tripedresser, not always of respectable character. "Was not thy mother a notorious tripe-wife?" demands Brome, in his "City Wit".

Trotters and cowheels are also mentioned in the literature of the past. Mayhew, in "London Labour", wrote: "For supper there is a sandwich, a meat pudding or a trotter." Cowheel, stewed so as to form a jelly, is recommended by Mouffet and Bennett: "A tender cowheel is counted restorative." Wesley advised, in 1747: "Take a cow-heel from the Tripe-house, ready drest."

The word "tripe" has been used to describe things with a supposed resemblance to tripe. "Tripe-velvet" or "Tripe de Velours" was an imitation of wool or thread, "mock" velvet, velveteen or fustian. A 1714 Book of Rates records: "Eighty tripes of velvet, per piece of 10 Ells, 3s 0d."

"Rock-tripe" or "Tripe de Roche" was an appellation given to various edible lichens in Canada which afforded a slightly nutritious but bitter and purgative food, as described by A Henry in his "Travels", published in 1809.

To souſe Pigs Feet and Ears.

CLEAN your Pigs Feet and Ears, and boil them 'till they are tender, then ſplit the Feet, and put them into Salt and Water with the Ears; when you uſe them, dry them well with a Cloth, and dip them in Batter made of Flour and Eggs, fry them a good Brown, and ſend them up with good melted Butter.

To souſe Tripe.

WHEN your Tripe is boiled, put it into Salt and Water, change the Salt and Water every Day 'till you uſe it, dip it in Batter, and fry it as the Pigs Feet and Ears, or boil it in freſh Salt and Water, with an Onion ſliced, and a few Sprigs of Parſley, and ſend melted Butter for Sauce.

To make Calves Foot Jelly.

PUT a Gang of Calf's Feet well cleaned into a Pan, with ſix Quarts of Water, and let them boil gently 'till reduced to two Quarts, then take out the Feet, ſcum off the Fat clean, and clear your Jelly from the Sediment, beat the whites of five Eggs to a Froth, then add one Pint of Liſbon, Madeira, or any pale made Wine, if you chuſe it, then ſqueeze in the Juice of three Lemons; when your Stock is boiling, take three Spoonfuls of it, and keep ſtirring it with your Wine and Eggs to keep it from curdling, then add a little more Stock, and ſtill keep ſtirring it, and then put it in the Pan, and ſweeten it with Loaf Sugar to your Taſte, a Glaſs of French Brandy will keep the Jelly from turning blue in froſty Air, put in the outer Rind of two Lemons, and let it boil one Minute all together, and pour it into a Flannel Bag, and let it run into a Baſon, and keep pouring it back gently into the Bag 'till it runs clear and bright, then ſet your Glaſſes under the Bag, and cover it leſt Duſt gets in.—If you would have the Jelly for a Fiſh Pond, Tranſparent Pudding, or Hen's Neſt, to be turned out of the Mould, boil half a Pound of Iſinglaſs in a Pint of Water, 'till reduced to one Quarter, and put it into the Stock before its refined.

From Elizabeth Raffald's "The Experienced English Housekeeper", published in Manchester in 1769 (Courtesy Chetham's Library)

The Nineteenth Century

Tripe has played its part in making the North and Midlands the Workshops of Britain. As the cotton trade grew in importance, mill hands did not have enough time or energy to cook meals in their homes during the week and tripe therefore became the ideal food - cheap but nourishing.

Tripe dressing was an acquired skill. In the Archives Department of Manchester Public Libraries there is a copy of an apprenticeship indenture (dated 27 January 1831), binding one Joseph Newton of Manchester, "a poor child of fourteen years", to James Lane, tripe dresser, also of Manchester.

However, it must be stated that conditions under which tripe dressing was carried out in the early nineteenth century were sometimes primitive to say the least. There were instances of tripe boiling being carried out in the kitchens and back yards of terraced cottages and other small premises hardly deserving the name "works".

J P Kay, in his book "The Moral and Physical Condition of the Working Classes", describes conditions that he found in some tripe houses of that period (1832). In a district of Manchester known as Irish Town, foul-smelling manufactories were situated side-by-side with dwelling houses. *"The Irk, black with the refuse of Dye-works erected upon its banks, receives ...drainage from the gas-works and filth of the most pernicious character, from bone-works, tanneries, size manufactories, etc."*

Magistrate's certificate which was attached to Joseph Newton's apprenticeship indenture

On the other side of the river, by Ducie Bridge, *"other tanneries, size manufactories and tripe houses occur. A series of courts occupies the other side, to which access is obtained by means of narrow, covered entries from Long Millgate."* In one of these courts (Allen's) were houses chiefly inhabited by silk and cotton weavers and winders, and each house contained in general three or four families.

An adjoining court (Barrett's), separated from Allen's Court only by a low wall, contained, besides a pigsty, *"a tripe manufactory in a low cottage, which was in a state of loathsome filth. Portions of animal matter were decaying in it, and one of the inner rooms was converted into a kennel and contained a litter of puppies. In the same court, on the opposite side, is a tan-yard, where skins are prepared...in open pits, and here also is a cat-gut manufactory. The offensive odour which arises from these areas cannot be conceived. Offal was allowed to accumulate with the grossest neglect of decency and disregard to the health of the surrounding inhabitants.*

Needless to say, the physical hazards consequent on living and working in such conditions are not difficult to imagine. A match-seller, seized with cholera on a Sunday, was dead by the following Wednesday, and not being buried until the Friday, five other cases of cholera were diagnosed on the day of his funeral. The next day seven more cases occurred, the day

1865 advertisement

after two more - these were nearly all fatal. There occurred others too, in spite of tardy efforts of the Board of Health to cleanse the area by fumigation and whitewashing all habitations of the courts."

The Public Health Act of 1875 designated the business of a tripe boiler (along with blood boiler, bone boiler, tallow melter and others) an "offensive trade", and as such it had to be regulated by local or urban district councils. In 1877 Kearsley UDC published a set of byelaws for tripe boilers, requiring them, at the close of every working day, to scrub down or otherwise cleanse all floors, walls and working surfaces; all refuse was to be collected and disposed of; the premises were to be kept in good repair, and, possibly the most important from the point of view of the inhabitants of the neighbouring houses, *"Every tripe-boiler shall adopt the best practicable means of rendering innocuous all vapours emitted during the process of boiling..."*

In addition, the entire building had to be hot lime-washed four times a year. The failure to observe all, or indeed any, of the byelaws made the offender liable to a fine of £5 or more - a not inconsiderable sum in the year 1877!

Local newspapers sometimes carried reports of court proceedings against erring tripe boilers. For example, at the turn of the century a Bolton man was brought before the local magistrates for causing "an obnoxious smell from a coal-fired boiler in Back Derby Street, to boil cows' belly, therefore causing a public nuisance."

The Twentieth Century

In recent history the aim of most tripedressers has been to ensure that a much-liked and nourishing food be prepared, cooked and served by up-to-date methods and upon hygienic principles, and sold at a price within the reach of everyone.

In 1909 proposals were made to bring a measure of unity into the trade. J S Hill, the head of an established Manchester firm, interested a group of like-minded tripedressers in pledging themselves to improve the status of the trade, which was by this time receiving commendation from the medical profession, dieticians and other food authorities. This co-operation worked to everyone's advantage and from these beginnings the UCP came into being in 1920.

For many years tripe shops had provided tables and chairs at which customers could eat a meal; sometimes there was a separate small dining room behind the shop. One such "supper bar" was to be found at Vose's tripe shop on Churchgate in Bolton.

With the emergence of larger companies, specially planned and fitted-out restaurants opened and were well-patronised by the public. One of the first of these new purpose-built eating places was in Burnley, opened by Mr Hill himself. Eventually, bright, clean and attractive shops appeared in most Lancashire towns, serving well-cooked meals in pleasant

1832 advertisement

Voses Restaurant on Market Street, Wigan

surroundings. The following delightful description of one such building comes from the Wigan Observer of 7th April 1917:

"NEW CAFE FOR WIGAN

The Tripe de Luxe Restaurant and Tea Room, which Messrs Vose and Son have opened at 8 Market Street, Wigan, was opened for business last Wednesday, after being thrown open for an informal inspection by the public, on Monday. The elaborate character of the appointments of the new cafe attracted attention...and the announcement that the Borough Magistrates had granted the new establishment a music licence for a permanent ladies' orchestra of three performers, also served to stimulate public interest.

On passing through the street door into a small vestibule with marble counters, which serves as a front shop, visitors at once pass on to the front dining-room, a spacious, well-lighted and handsomely decorated apartment, on the floor of which stand the white-clothed tables and the seating, accommodation of the chamber being about 300.

This room, which is called the general restaurant ... has panelled walls with oak divisions. The furniture is of the Early English style, combining dignity and beauty. At the rear is the servery, where all utensils used are treated with hot, sterilised water, none of the vessels being actually handled in the process.

Lavatory accommodation is also provided on the most scientific lines. A handsome stairway, modelled on the manner of the eighteenth century, gives access to the Tea Room on the first floor, and it is in this apartment that the ladies' orchestra dispenses music. Daintily placed palms and other patches of greenery give a cool relief to the general colourings of the apartment, which are quite tasteful and effective, being of a delicate pink relieved with enrichments in old ivory. Taking all the decorations together, there is a splendid sense of openness and harmony about the whole establishment, together with an old world charm, delicacy and refinement.

Messrs Vose and Son, to whose enterprise Wigan owes this interesting addition to its catering attractions, are noted purveyors, and the arrangements for supplying their future customers with the highest class bill of fare could not be excelled. The structural arrangements have been excellently carried out by Messrs Waring and Gillow of Manchester, and the entire premises...fitted with electric light."

Regrettably, this elegant establishment was closed down a few years ago.

The tripe trade flourished up to and during the First World War, but then came the slump and the great Depression. Lancashire's industrial output slowed down and unemployment became a grim reality to many.

By 1920 it was realised by the tripe dressers of Manchester and district that a number of separate firms could not be operated as efficiently or as economically as one large concern, which would have obvious advantages in buying and in the co-ordination of supply to the retail shops. All these separate interests were therefore amalgamated and this consolidation was the beginning of the food production and distribution combine now known as the UCP (United Cattle Products).

Depression hung like a cloud over the Lancashire towns in the 1920s and 1930s. Trade everywhere was bad but, partly through judicious advertising and partly because of the continuing cheapness of the products, tripe and cowheel remained popular sources of nourishment.

A perusal of trade directories for this period shows how widespread tripe shops were. For example, the 1923 directory gives 21 names in Burnley; the Preston directory for 1926-7 lists 35; Stockport had over 50 listed and in 1925 there were 16 tripe dealers in Wigan. Bolton's directory for 1922 lists over 40 tripe dealers, several with more than one shop, and ten years later there were only slightly fewer.

George Hough started his tripedressing business in Audenshaw and went on to become general manager of Arnold & Hough. The business subsequently became part of the UCP

Part 2

From Abattoir to Factory

In its natural state, tripe is part of the stomach of the ox; the tissue between the lining and the more muscular structure. There are several different kinds, according to the part of the animal from which they are taken, and these are given various names such as blanket or double, honeycomb, monk's hood and book or reed.

From a chemical point of view, tripe contains a fair amount of protein and a large amount of connective tissue, which is transformed into gelatine on boiling, thus making the fibres digestible. It also contains a quantity of fat, although this is not diffused throughout and some is removed during the preparation. The basic substance of meat juice, creatinine, is also to be found, along with glycogen (animal starch) and sarolactic, a milky substance.

So tripe contains valuable body-building material and it has long been recommended for invalids, people of weak digestion and others on light diets. It is very light, has the same nutritional value in B vitamins and protein as stewed beef and takes a third of the time to digest – it is the most easily digested of all solid animal foods.

Tripes and cowheels come from abattoirs as far away as the

Tripe dressing in the 1930s

North of Scotland, and some are even imported, deep frozen, when the home supply is insufficient. On arrival at the factory they are hung up, cut open and thoroughly inspected. The insides are usually a dirty-looking blackish-yellow or brown, depending on whether the beasts were fed on hay or barley. If the animals had been out to grass, chlorophyll would have dyed the stomachs and this is difficult, if not impossible, to remove. Sometimes hay is given a day or so before they are slaughtered, which goes some way towards removing the green tint.

"People tend to think the tripe is 'off', but this is not the case, and over-bleaching takes away some of the food value and flavour," I was told by one tripedresser. "Green" tripe is usually used in animal and pet foods. Cows' tripes, tough and yellow, are also now used mostly in pet foods.

Rust can be found in the stomach should the animal have swallowed a metal object, and cysts and other irregularities can also lead to the discarding of the animal product.

Each tripedressing firm has its own method of cleaning and preparing tripe, but the end product is the same. In its natural state tripe is covered with an impervious skin envelope, which preserves the purity of the tripe and which must be peeled off before the delicate white tissue is exposed. Tripe needs to be washed out and scalded several times, and then it requires six or seven hours boiling to make it tender. Regional variations in boiling time account for variations in the time required for cooking given in different cookery books; some state one hour, while others will give five or six hours for the same dish. Northern tripe is sold already cooked, but in parts of Scotland and the South it is only par-boiled and requires further cooking at home.

At the factory the tripes are first placed in a large washing machine which tumbles them round in a solution of lime and soda, almost at boiling point. After about twenty minutes the hot water is drained off and

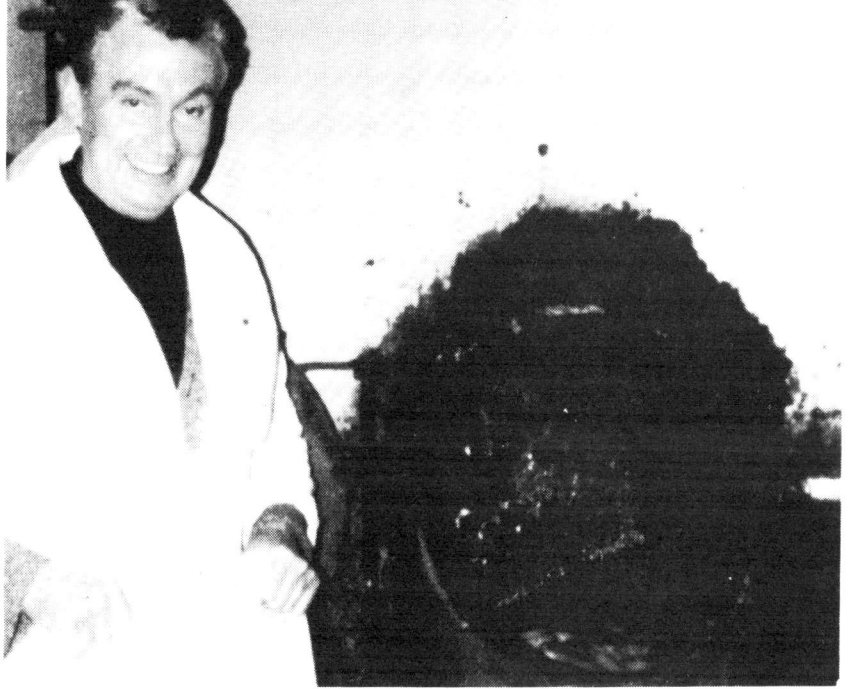

Reg Coburn and a preliminary cleaning machine at Parry Scragg's works, Liverpool

the machine is refilled with cold water to cool down the contents, which by this time have a nice clean look. The effect of this first process is to soften the tripes and draw out the colouring matter; it also loosens the membrane on the insides of the stomach and fat is drawn off. (The fat is later sold as tallow.)

The tripes are then placed in a smaller machine, six at a time, and churned around in an abrasive chamber to take off the "rind" or thin outer skin. This process was formerly done by hand, but nowadays "La Parmentiere" machine does the job very efficiently and far quicker. Some tripedressers, however, maintain that the old way with "dandy" brushes was better and more professional.

From here the tripes are transferred to large vats, where they are cooked for two or three hours, depending on the age of the animal. After this process is completed they are placed in "becks" to be bleached white in a weak peroxide solution. This also has the effect of "plumping" or expanding the tripe. Finally, they are left in cold water to rinse off the bleach and to give texture to the finished product. The following day the tripe is ready to be "dressed" - looked over and edged to give an attractive appearance before going out on sale.

Other Products

COWHEELS. Sold ready-cooked, cowheels can make a tasty

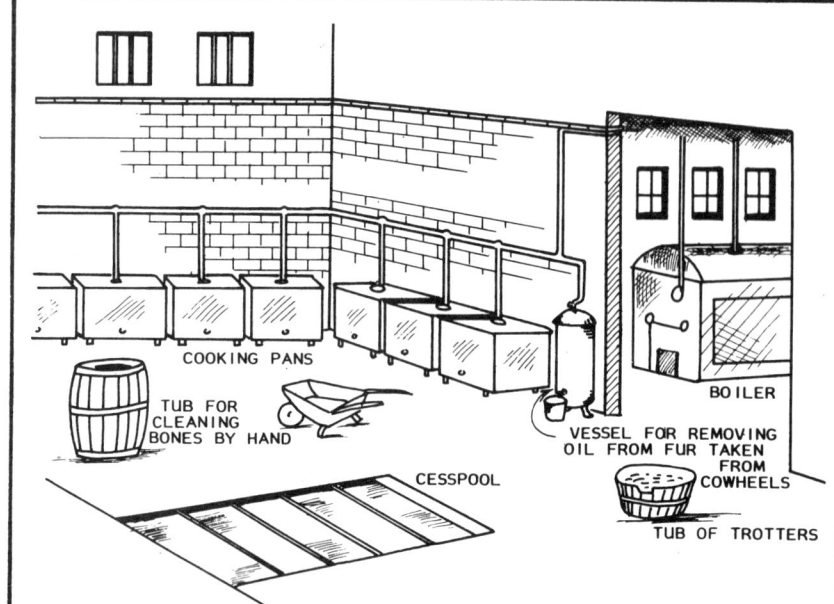

Inside the Silverwell Lane tripe works, Bolton

snack or be used in stews and pies. Cowheels make a good gravy and the jelly-producing substance is invaluable for brawns and potted meats.

The cows' feet are washed clean in their raw state, again by machine, and then cut a certain way to enable the oil to flow from the foot whilst they are boiling. After boiling for three or four hours with the hide on, they are cooled down and the hair peeled off ("Just like peeling an orange") and then they are bleached white in the same manner as the tripe.

SHEEP'S TROTTERS are cooked in the same way as tripe, and bleached white.

PIGS' TROTTERS (or pigs' feet) are also cooked for about two hours, but not bleached.

FAT emerging from the boiling of tripes is an important by-product, being essentially edible. It is refined and sold in bulk for many purposes, and is equal to the finest home-made dripping.

NEATSFOOT OIL is yet another nutritious product. It is a perfect oil for the cooking of fish and chips and can be used in salad dressings. Neatsfoot oil is also used as a rubbing oil for aches and pains; in soap-making, and nowadays it is used underwater on North Sea oil rigs.

CALF'S FOOT JELLY. The gelatinous substance found in cowheels and trotters prepared by the tripedresser was at one time quite a common form of nourishment advised for invalids.

ELDER (the cow's udder) is another form of food, yellow in colour and firm in texture, like cooked meat. It is boiled for around 12 hours, dressed to look edible, and sold without bleaching.

BONES were sent for bonemeal; HOOVES sent to the glue factory.

TALLOW, made from the fat "leavings" in the cesspool or draining pit where the excess water and offal is collected up, is used as a lubricant in the making of soap, and in leather dressing. It was once used to make tallow candles, a process superseded by the method of making candles from fatty acids derived from the tallow.

"Nothing is wasted" is a comment frequently made, and from the above, I can well believe it!

Imported French scraping machines

Part 3
The Principal Combines
Parry Scragg Ltd

This firm was founded by Frank Parry, who bought a tripe works in Carruthers Street, Liverpool, around 1922. A limited company, F D Parry (Milk-meat) Ltd, was formed in 1927 and tripe was dressed in the same building for over 60 years.

In 1975 Parry Scragg Ltd was formed, with a 50% shareholding of F D Parry Ltd and 50% of Scragg (North Western) Ltd. The amalgamation with the Scragg company (itself over 100 years old) was brought about by a Compulsory Purchase Order being served on Scragg's premises in Borax Street, Liverpool, compelling them to look for alternative accommodation.

When the two firms merged they extended the Carruthers Street works, bought the present factory in 1979, and at the time of writing are looking at other property, with a view to further expansion.

About 18 people are employed inside the works, and self-employed franchise agents obtain sales in Scotland, the Midlands and the South. There is a van delivery service to the Lake District in the North, and down to Crewe, the Potteries and Bangor in North Wales.

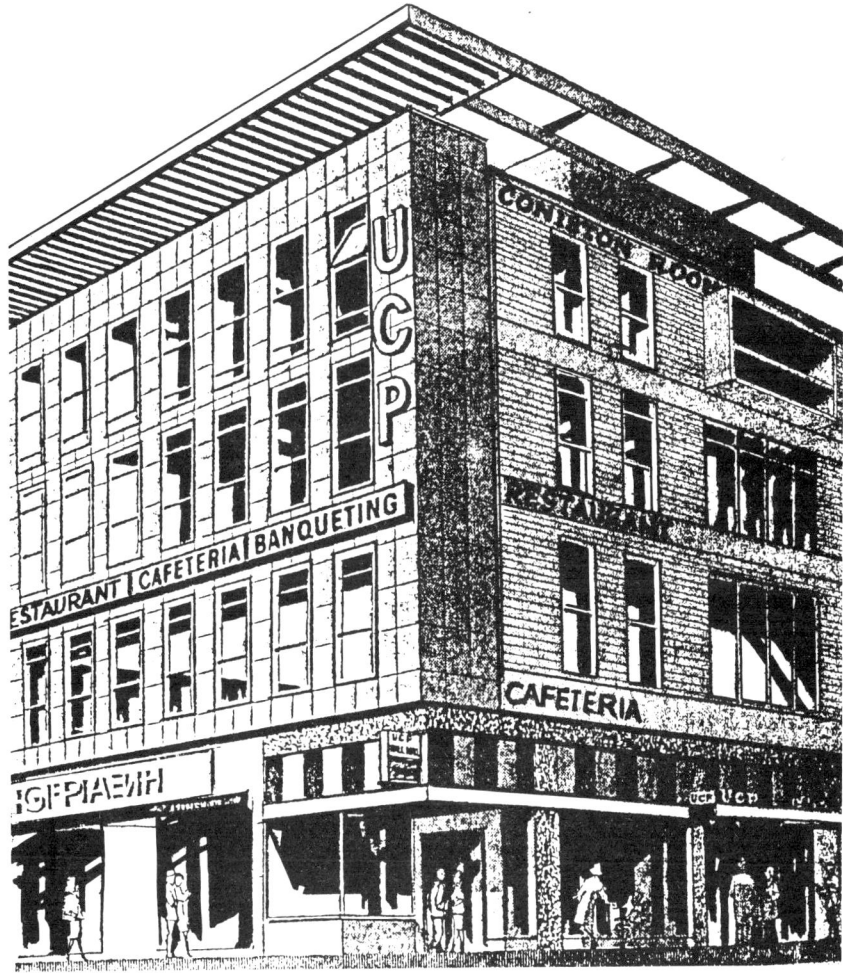

The UCP restaurant on the corner of Market Street and Pall Mall, Manchester

Mr Shiach, the Managing Director of Parry Scragg, commented that in a rough line stretching between Glasgow and Edinburgh people are now buying English, or cooked, tripe. There was a time when they would only purchase "raw" tripe and prepare it themselves. In the Border region there is no demand at all, and in Cumbria and Northumberland there is a winter trade only. Conversely, in Lancashire and Yorkshire the emphasis is on summer trade.

In the South, a Brighton firm has no trade in summer and has to lay off workers until business starts up in the winter. So although there is some demand for the product in other areas of Britain, it is in Lancashire and Yorkshire where the main sales tradition exists.

In the old days, clogs and sacking aprons were worn, but nowadays Parry Scragg's employees wear wellingtons and blue boiler suits at the "dirty" end of the works and white boiler suits at the "clean" end. They also have large rubber aprons, covering the whole front of the body, which can be easily washed down after the day's work.

Approximately 1,700 ox bellies are processed by Parry Scragg every week, even more in the summer months, and around one and a quarter million gallons of water is used every year – the company's water bill amounts to more than the fuel bill (lighting, heating and fuel oils combined)!

Mr Shiach predicts that the

trade will probably change direction in the future, with tripe being prepared in sauces and meat products similar to pates, used as a filler for sandwiches and canned as ready meals. "At present there are only about seven abattoirs killing more than a thousand cattle a week, and we are now in competition with other tripe-eating countries such as France, Belgium, Spain, Portugal and Nigeria."

United Cattle Products

The UCP has been well known in the Greater Manchester and Lancashire areas for upwards of 65 years. Today the company mainly supplies wholesalers, although there are still several tripe stalls in local markets owned or managed by the UCP.

The UCP was formed in 1920 with the amalgamation of some 15 Lancashire tripedressers, such as J S Hill's, Ralph Mason of Burnley, Cox of Bury and Vose of Bolton. The rapid growth of the combination led to the building of new hygienic factories, such as those at Levenshulme (1927) and Monton (1938). The head offices of the enterprise were in Manchester.

The bulk of the company's production was at first sold to individual retailers, giving them the advantages of guaranteed quality and continuity of supply.

Fifty years after the formation of the UCP, long serving employee Fred Wetters recalled his early years in the trade. He went to work for a Stockport tripedresser in 1915 and began his day by collecting the post and picking up orders from two shops – the first from under a stone in the yard and the second from under a vinegar bottle on the counter!

The UCP also advised retailers on improving or reorganising their businesses; free advertising was provided in the form of showcards and recipe books. The firm expanded into other fields, such as pie making, meat, fish, poultry and delicatessen products. The UCP flourished in the North of England, although it has campaigned in the South, trying to persuade housewives there that tripe is good for digestion and the domestic budget.

UCP tripe is sold "perfectly cooked", ready for serving. The firm's advertising emphasised the savings in fuel costs and, "There are no bones to waste –

you buy a pound and eat a pound."

New UCP depots were usually planned with dining rooms behind the shops, where hot and cold meals could be obtained. These became landmarks in Lancashire, with their warm, red-painted fronts – "in order to brighten up the grey streets!" – and the famous oval sign. There were UCP cafes and restaurants in Manchester, Blackpool, Southport, Oldham, Bolton, Macclesfield, Rochdale, Bury, Stockport, Wigan and many other towns, each assuring quality, comfort and "no fancy prices".

The Market Street Restaurant (Hill's) in Manchester was for fifty years one of the UCP's best-known eating houses. In June 1964 the company opened another restaurant in Pall Mall.

The following description comes from the Manchester Evening News:

"Soft music and pleasant surroundings induce a relaxed atmosphere. With the accent on comfort, you can enjoy a three-course meal for only 4s. The restaurant itself can seat 160 and is open from 11.30am until 6.30pm.

Features on this floor are the large windows overlooking Manchester's busy Market Street, the neat cloakroom and the soft browns and oranges of the decor...

Hundreds of hot and nourishing lunches will be served every day in the cafeteria. Glass doors open into this spacious section of the building where customers can use the self-service facilities and get a tremendously wide choice of meals.

1940s showcard

Dominating the cafeteria is a giant panel depicting a country landscape with trees, fields and a river. The panel was designed and executed in Italy and covers most of the wall. It is illuminated in bright and cheerful colours.

Immediately beneath it is yet another unusual feature of this ultra-modern premises. It is a fountain and miniature waterfall in a natural rock setting with artificial flowers and ferns.

Above the self-service counters and the coffee bar in the cafeteria are cedar shingle canopies, and the lighting, like everything else, has been carefully thought out. As well as meals, diners in the cafeteria can enjoy a coffee, soft drinks, or an ice-cream at prices to suit the pocket.

One of the most impressive highlights is the banqueting suite on the top floor. Completely self-contained, it can cater for 120 people comfortably. In the Coniston Suite, as it is called, there is every facility to make a party or an important reception a success. Again the decor is superb. Most of one wall has

been faced with Westmorland green stone, while on the other side of the large dining room is a wall covered with blue animal hide.

Just off the main dining room in the Coniston Suite is a reception room with a bar; the dance floor is of maple wood and the lighting is housed in ceiling recesses. Amplifiers are set in the ceiling so that speeches or music can be heard in every corner of the room. Behind the bar is yet another Italian-made 'back cloth'; this time a scene to match the Coniston theme has been chosen.

Behind the scenes ... are the equally important kitchens, equipped with the very latest refrigeration systems and stainless steel units, and are mainly electric. On the ground floor are UCP's shop, butchery and self-service store. The bright and modern shop sells the products which have made UCP famous..."

In 1970 the UCP celebrated its Golden Jubilee. Fifty years of selling tripe, cowheels and trotters had tended to produce a "beer and braces" image, but

1920s advertisement

the Chairman of the company announced: "The image of the UCP as tripedressers is being changed and though the sound foundation has been maintained, we accept that change is inevitable and we are moving with the times." He went on to say that the new Oyster Catcher Restaurant in Blackpool was a trendsetter for the catering side of the business.

In 1970 tripe sales averaged about 50 tons a week, compared with 200 tons before the Second World War. "People now have far more foods to choose from, but tripe will always have its devotees..." In 1972 the whole company moved to Monton.

In 1975 it was reported that staff at a Spanish restaurant in Manchester had volunteered to sample the old Lancashire delicacy, which was soon to be exported to their homeland. (UCP won the export order because of a lull in the Spanish tripe trade.) One of the restaurant proprietors said that in Spain they tended to cook tripe sauces, with tomatoes, paprika or chillies, or make a stew with chick peas and tripe. His partner declared with a smile, "Tripe is very much like a woman in the morning; the way the English eat it is like a woman half awake and falling out of bed. The Spanish way, it's as if she's put on her make-up and made herself ready for the day..."

I visited the tripe stall on Salford Food Market in the company of Mr Hill, the present Managing Director of the UCP. The manageress, Joan Dobson, sells, in addition to the usual honeycomb, "jelly" and "black" tripe, elder, pig's belly, cowheel, black puddings and other products. Most of her customers buy tripe to eat plain with tomatoes, or stewed with onions, and in the summer months she has known four-year-olds come to buy tripe and elder!

Although the shops might have gone, tripe and cowheels are still readily available in market stalls and butchers' shops throughout the North.

Cox's tripe shop on the corner of Broad Street and Haymarket Street, Bury

Some Tripedressers Past and Present

KRM Products

This is a small family firm in Todmorden, begun in 1876. Before his death in 1983, Mr Ken Hemingway, father of the present proprietor, recalled how orders were delivered into Lancashire by horse and cart. Then came Ford Model T flat wagons, and today there are modern vans, lined with fibreglass for hygiene.

About 20 years ago there were some 350 tripe firms, large and small, thoughout the country; today KRM Products is one of about 30 survivors. (The North West Membership of the Tripedressers' Association in 1984 was about 8.) Mr Hemingway thought it unlikely, however, that the trade would die out altogether; there will always be a good demand for tripe.

The Todmorden premises are small and compact, all processes being carried out as in the bigger companies, and there is a fair turnover of tripe products. It is principally a wholesale business, selling mainly tripe in the summer months and cowheels in winter.

In the processing KRM use lime and soda (with the occasional addition of a very dilute ammonia solution) and deal in the usual products, including black tripe or "scragg", pigs' belly, pigs' feet and dripping. The raw tripes are obtained from various sources, but mainly from the Leeds slaughterhouse.

The company's vans carry the slogan "KRM Products for Quality

1896 advertisement for a Bury firm of tripedressers

Tripe" and deliver to such Lancashire towns as Blackburn, Bolton, Preston, Swinton, Wigan and Manchester. Tripe is also exported to Nigeria, the West Indies, Spain, France and Poland.

Richard Byrne Ltd

This Blackburn firm was started by the grandfather of the present proprietor over a hundred years ago, and became a limited company in 1912. Richard Byrne had previously worked for William Almond, at that time probably the largest tripedressing firm in Lancashire, with works in Blackburn, Wigan and Preston. Other Blackburn tripedressers at that time were George Monk and Robert S Baines. (William Almond and George Monk joined the UCP in the immediate post-war years.) Blackburn also had a well-known itinerant tripeseller in the early part of this century – "Tripe Dick". I wonder if anyone in Blackburn still remembers him?

Since Richard Byrne was the last on the scene, as it were, there were no supplies of offal to be obtained locally, or indeed from anywhere within a reasonable distance. Supplies were brought by rail from Aberdeen (William Murray), Edinburgh (Hide & Skin Company), Glasgow (John Brown) and Eastriggs (George Veevers).

If there was any need to make an alteration to the company's standing order with a supplier, a telegram despatched to, say, Aberdeen by 11.00am on Monday would result in the goods being delivered by noon Tuesday. The train would leave Aberdeen late Monday, discharging and collecting its various wagons in the marshalling yards of Edinburgh, Glasgow and Carlisle. The order would be shunted into Blackburn Goods Yard and the final stage would be completed by horse-drawn lorry. Richard Byrne Ltd would have been advised of the delivery either by telegram on Monday evening, or postcard by first post (7.00am) Tuesday!

Hill & Hiley

In 1883 Frederick Hill started a tripe dressing business in Salford. He was a distant relative of J S Hill, head of the tripe firm founded in Ardwick and mentioned earlier in connection with the UCP. Frederick Hill's first shop was on Regent Road, Salford, and in the years up to the First World War he acquired other retail outlets in Salford and Hulme. The tripe works was in Rennie Street, off Regent Road.

For a brief period in the 1920s, Hill's advertised their tripe on posters on the sides of trams – "Millions now living will never die if they eat Hill's tripe." The posters were withdrawn following objections from a prominent religious organisation!

Mrs Nellie Jones worked for Hill's in a one storey building, "rather like a big shed, painted

1913 advertisement

white; there were pigs and poultry kept on land at the back." Working hours were from 6.00am until 5.30pm, with three quarters of an hour for lunch. Nellie was a good dresser. She wore a white blouse with long sleeves, generally pinned back at the elbows. She never had rheumatism, but she had a lot of colds in winter. During the winter the employees often had to break ice to get at the tripe on starting work in the mornings, and sometimes their clogs would stick to the duckboards on which they stood to dress the tripe. Because of the grease in the tripe, Nellie had lovely

soft hands ("Didn't need no Fairy Liquid!")

Once, at a time when wages were 17/- a week, the women wanted a raise. They were reluctant to approach Mr Hill for a long time, but one day Nellie was elected as spokeswoman. They got their raise - about 6d a week!

"Father liked thick seam done in milk and onions with potatoes and carrots, also cowheel stew with onions, carrots and a pennorth o' pot-herbs - when it was cold it went like jelly - and he had elder on his sandwiches for packed lunches."

Alderman J S Hill, Mayor of Manchester 1942/43

The Hiley tripedressing firm was founded in 1866 by Allan Hiley on Oldfield Road, Salford. In the last decade of the nineteenth century, Allan's son, Beaumont Hiley, started his own business in Eccles. Today, behind a chemist's shop on Church Street, down a narrow passage known as Hall's Buildings, there are the remains of a sixteenth century building. This had been converted into three cottages by the time Beaumont Hiley arrived, and it was in a wash boiler in the end cottage that he first began boiling tripe. In the early 1900s a shop fronting Hall's Buildings, on Church Street, was acquired and converted into a cafe and shop by the family.

Allan and George Hiley, grandsons of the founder, succeeded to the business in the years before the First World War, by which time the family had a works on Chaney Street in Pendleton.

George Hiley, a well-built man, over six feet tall, was a prominent figure in Eccles. He became Mayor and in his day was the only living Freeman of the town. He was introduced to King George VI and Queen Elizabeth when they visited Lancashire soon after the Coronation, and George's daughter can still remember how nervous she felt about having to curtsey to the Royal couple!

Of George's six children, five were involved in the trade. Frank, born in 1904 and the youngest son, began by weighing out orders at their Chaney Street works. He recalls how their products were delivered by horse and cart to begin with. "But father got two ponies

"A POEM IN GREEN AND SILVER"

A VISIT TO THE NEW HILEY'S— NOW OPEN—

IS AN EVENT for those who prefer delicious food — spotless appointments — fragrant coffee — dainty lunches — teas or suppers in real luxury, yet at most economical prices.

THE PLACE TO MEET YOUR FRIENDS WHEN IN ECCLES—EAT AT HILEY'S

DELICIOUS COOKED FOODS

Hiley's are famous for pure cooked foods. At the RETAIL COUNTER can be purchased an array of cooked foods ready for quick, appetising meals in the home.

A Branch of FREDk. HILL and HILEY LTD.

TAKE SOMETHING HOME FROM HILEY'S

THE BRIGHT SPOT OF ECCLES

1937 newspaper advertisement

for me, as he considered a horse might be too big for a young lad to handle." Another of Frank's chores was to pick up bellies from the Water Street abattoir in Manchester. During the First World War, when his elder brothers were serving in the army, he went to school part time, delivering tripe in the morning and attending school in the afternoon.

Frank's sister Lucy started work at 9.00am, first in the works' office and later supervising retail outlets on Broad Street and Cross Lane, Salford; in Moss Side, Cadishead, and of course the Eccles shop. She had time off during the day, but would often be out late at night with the directors, checking that everything was in order and that the shops were properly cleaned out after the day's trading. She was also responsible for staffing.

In June 1936 the firms of Frederick Hill and Hiley's became subsidiaries of the UCP combine, and in order to cope with increasing trade a decision was made to build a new factory. Four acres of land were acquired at Monton, Eccles, and the first sod was cut by Alderman George Hiley, then Mayor of Eccles.

Lucy remembers the care which was taken to display their products: *"The shop windows were set out very attractively, with sprigs of parsley and tomato as garnishing. In winter there was a great demand for trotters and cowheels, whilst in summer tripe was popular."* On the day following the Manchester Blitz in 1941 she remembers going to inspect the damage. Several shop windows had been

1929 advertisement

blown in by bomb blast, which meant they had to be boarded up, usually for the duration of the war.

Frank and Lucy were never very fond of tripe, although Lucy admitted to a partiality for a dish of steak and cowheel...

Entwistle's

This was a well-known family firm in Ashton under Lyne. The works and cold stores were in Conduit Street. The firm was started in 1850 by Richard Entwistle, who formed the company Richard Entwistle & Sons. One of the sons married Maria Arnold, the daughter of his main competitor, which caused quite a furore at the time and her family refused to have anything further to do with her! The firm continued

under three generations of Entwistles until 1947, when another Richard Entwistle, grandson of the founder, retired and sold out. He died in 1975, aged 90.

Alfred Entwistle, Richard's son, tells the following anecdote about his grandfather: *"It was the custom in those days to have competitions in local pubs and other meeting places at weekends. A competition might be for 'The Biggest Celery' or 'The Best Rose', that sort of thing. One day a regular market customer asked Grandfather to provide him with the biggest cowheel he could find for his local 'do'. So Grandfather singled out a hind-foot from a Hereford ox, and tying a string round it, so the foot would not go astray among a boiling of 40 to 50 'gang' (there were four feet to a gang), he began to process it for the competition. Grandfather made a strong mixture of soda and lime in warm water and immersed the ox-heel in the solution overnight. (The solution was so strong that it brought the zinc coating off the bath!)*

The week after the competition, Grandfather asked his customer how he had fared. The man replied, 'They banned it, and said it must have come from another animal!' The 'blowing' in the soda and lime solution had been TOO successful!"

Working hours at Richard Entwistle & Sons depended on the workload; being a small private firm there were no fixed hours. Normally there was an early start, half past seven or earlier, according to the day, and very often the work continued late, sometimes until midnight. After the market stalls closed on Saturdays it would be 10.00pm by the time

Mrs Sarah (Sally) Entwistle at her tripe stall on Ashton Market

the returns had been brought back to the works.

The Wellington Road shop, where Alfred and his brother Richard were born, was open until 11.45 on Saturday nights. *"On the opposite side of the counter were big mirrors, and there was a little narrow counter where people could stand and eat their tripe from little plates. Until 1939 some shops stayed open till twelve at night, Saturday and Sunday included."*

Richard recalled: *"There were six tripe stalls on the market, and we ended up with five out of the six (the UCP had the other one). We also had a shop in Warrington Street, and in my grandfather's day there was an Entwistle's shop in Hooley Hill and also one on Cavendish Street. Even after he'd retired to Blackpool, Grandfather sold tripe, because so many Ashton people visiting Blackpool asked him for it. We would send him a supply on the goods train every week and he'd sell it from his home!"*

Alfred and Richard's father had a fine factory built of Accrington brick, complete with a tall chimney, and it was considered to be the best tripe works in the district. There were originally about 20 workers, including young Alfred and Richard and two carters, but just after the War there were about a dozen.

In addition to their own shops and stalls, Entwistle's were also suppliers to the trade. At one time they obtained their offal from local abattoirs, but gradually these slaughterhouses closed down as the industry became centralised. Tripes from Scottish abattoirs were of very good quality and in demand. In later years, most of Entwistle's tripes came from the Argentine and were put into cold stores,

> TRIPE: Tripe and cow-heels are already perfectly cooked. Instead of burning black diamonds in hours of cooking you can serve tripe and cow-heels hot in a few minutes. Fuel, work and time saved. Tripe 9d. per lb.; cow-heels 4d. per lb.

Entwistle advertisement dating from 1926

some to be re-sold to other dressers.

The preparation of tripe products requires the skills of a master tripedresser; someone who knows what he will get when the meat is still on the hoof, and also knows something of the butchering trade. When the business changed hands in 1947, Alfred and Richard, with their understanding of all the processes, continued as managers for the new owners.

Richard pointed out: *"Unless you know how to turn it out; how to assess the approximate temperature of the water, for example, and how it is going to be in seven or eight hours' time – and we're talking of hundreds of gallons – you could be in trouble. That is where inexperienced tripe cooks go wrong. My father was an expert. When we had a vat of tepid water ready to stand the tripes in overnight, he could put his hand in it and say, 'Two buckets o'boiling water in that an' it'll be right!' You see, when tripe is left in solution overnight it generates its own heat, and some people cannot calculate that."*

Presentation of the product was an important factor: *"Some people nowadays don't know how to handle what we call a belly of*

Richard Entwistle

tripe. The worst offenders are butchers – they know all about red meat, but the white offal, which is our speciality, is a mere sideline to them. For instance, they don't realise that the seam is supposed to be divided up by skilful manipulation of the knife, cutting it and splaying it out so as to give more of the flat tripe. Once, on the market stall, we had a pound of tripe over and four people came up, each wanting a quarter. Father cut it into four equal parts, and believe me that's not easy, for you should give about an inch of seam to a pound of tripe, widening out as you cut."

There was an art in the setting out and the handling of tripe; someone would be eating the product and so it should be treated with respect. Mrs Entwistle did this beautifully, according to her sons: *"How well a colour photograph of our Wellington Road shop would look today, set out as we used to have it, with tripe and tomatoes, and everything nicely ticketed, so that each product in the window was a little star in its own right. For instance, there was 'English Elder', 'Delicious Honeycomb Tripe' and 'Lambs' Trotters'. In one corner was a sign: 'Doctor's Report: If people knew the strength and support in tripe they would certainly eat more'."*

Mrs Entwistle coined the phrase: "If you would live to an age that is ripe, eat plenty of Entwistle's wholesome tripe." This slogan was printed on tram tickets to boost trade. Large, gas-filled balloons with "Entwistle's Tripe" printed on them were given to each child whose parent had made a purchase, and who could recite the slogan. About fifty of the balloons were released on

Entwistle's tripe being advertised in North Africa during the Second World War

Ashton Moss, all bearing a trade ticket and address, and the promise of £1 to the sender of the balloon reaching the farthest point from Ashton. The winning entry was returned from Wales.

Among the many recipes are tripe and onions ("Tripes a la mode de Caen" is a posh version, according to Alfred), stewed tripe with mashed potatoes, scalloped tripe, tripe au gratin, tripe in celery sauce, ragout of tripe, cowheel pie and tripe wiggle. Alfred prefers the unbleached tripe, which is difficult to obtain these days. *"The very process of bleaching tends to 'blow' the tripe, putting weight, which is really only water, into it. (They do the same thing with ham.) We used to specialise in the unbleached tripe - they used to call it 'the special'. True tripe gourmets actually prefer their tripe and cowheels to be unbleached - the taste is the test! A plate of unbleached tripe with plenty of seam, and chips, that's my favourite!"* Alfred is also partial to sliced elder, browned on each side in the frying pan, with bacon.

Richard has his own favourite - tripe salad. This consists of half a pound of tripe (again unbleached), a couple of slices of elder, the thick end of the "slag" - the "leaf" or black tripe - and a tomato. *"You can also add some nice crisp lettuce and spring onions, but there's a plate to give you a substantial meal. You wouldn't need anything else and it'd do you good!"*

Entwistle advertisement printed on a tram ticket, c1925

He gave his recipe for tripe and onions: Put a medium-sized onion, diced, into a pan of boiling water for 10 or 15 minutes till soft, then add half a pound of cooked tripe, cut into one inch squares, salt and pepper, perhaps a knob or two of butter, top-of-the-milk and a spoonful of cornflour. Simmer until the onion is cooked through and you can put a fork into the tripe, and the dish is ready. This would make a good, nourishing meal for two people.

"The decline of the trade is not explained away by one factor alone," asserts Richard. *"Where there are problems there are more contributing elements than one first realises. Since the* last War there has been an influx of cooked meats and other delicacies; one could buy tripe off the ration during the wartime years, so people were glad to try other products."* Another factor was marketing, or the lack of it; tripe never had modern marketing techniques applied to it. *"My brother put forward one or two ideas, and we had special cards displayed in our retail outlets, reading: 'Entwistle's Tripe for People of Taste'. That slogan did us quite a lot of good."*

Entwistle's old No.3 stall on Ashton Market is still selling tripe.

The tripe dressing firm of Arnold's, in Arnold Street, Richard Entwistle's main competitor in the early years, was taken over by the UCP in 1920 and the premises were rebuilt. A former employee, Harry Sutcliffe, recalled: *"Before the 1920s it was a very dirty job, but they modernised it and lined the walls with white tiled bricks, which cost about 1/6d each to lay."*

At the beginning of the War production was transferred to the UCP works at Rochdale. The Arnold Street works was used again for a short time after the war but soon closed.

Briggs' Tripe Works

This old-established Manchester firm is now owned by Peter Briggs: *"The firm was founded in 1898 by my great-grandfather, Absalom Briggs, who brought his business over from Halifax by horse and cart. He opened a shop opposite the Osborne Theatre on Oldham Road, where he prepared and sold tripe. In course of time, as the business*

The 70-foot chimney of Arnold's Tripe Works being demolished in May 1962

extended, his son Fred found larger premises in Viaduct Street, Beswick, from where he supplied other shops, again by means of horse transport."

The present factory in Newton Heath was built in 1922, and another shop, 47 Church Street, Newton Heath, was purchased. Peter's father, Leslie Briggs, was brought up with his brother and sisters at this shop. When Leslie and his brother started working, the hours were from 7.00am to 11.00pm. Peter himself began in the business in 1953 at the age of 15, and at that time there were ten employees; today there are just three.

Peter's work entailed de-hairing the cowheels, scraping cows' bellies, collecting raw tripes from the Water Street abattoir (a job he hated!), general cleaning duties and delivering to shops, in addition to keeping their own shop well supplied. The shop was then run by Peter's aunts, who were kept busy selling tripe, cowheels, sheep's trotters, elder and neatsfoot oil.

Throughout the 1950s tripe was still popular, and there being an insufficient supply of bellies locally, Briggs imported from Australia and Brazil, and obtained cowheels from Aberdeen.

Peter took over the running of the firm in the 1960s, and expanded into other lines, such as black puddings, which they made themselves, roast chicken,

pies and so on. A shop in Blackley village, which had been theirs originally, was kept going by a crippled old lady. "She hadn't been outside the door for twenty years; her life was selling the odd quarter of tripe or half a cowheel." When she died, Briggs took the shop over, but barely three years later the building was demolished.

The 1970s brought about other diversifications and a retraction in the labour force. The inevitable decline in business made it necessary to begin manufacturing other products. And the reason for the decline? "I believe it is the availability of so many other fast foods, such as beefburgers and pizzas, and of course the older generation of traditional tripe eaters is dying out..."

Peter doesn't find it easy to state his own preference among tripe dishes. He likes it curried, fried with bacon, and in winter the ubiquitous tripe and onions. "But for all the fancy ways, there's nothing to beat cold, fresh tripe, with plenty of salt and vinegar, and a nice English tomato!"

Worsick's of Colne

This was a well-known family firm, run by Harold Worsick, his sister Elizabeth and a labourer, Paddy. Harold's widow, Mrs Isabel Worsick (who

Miss Elizabeth (Libby) Worsick, Harold's sister

was born in 1896), described their life:

"Harold used to do the tripe dressing at our cooking place at the bottom of Buck Street, near the Nags Head in Windy Bank. Paddy lived across from the cooking place and worked for Harold all his life. The Nags Head and all the houses have been pulled down now.

Our goods originally came from the Argenta company - Harold liked their tripe - and then we bought from Leeds abattoirs. The tripe, trotters and elder all had to be washed and scrubbed, boiled and simmered until tender, and then put into round, real oak tubs. I used to dress them, getting all the skin and fur off, before they were put in another big tub with water and ice. (The tubs came from Whittaker's of Leeds.) The tripe was lifted out of the tub and put in more ice, in three big zinc baths about six feet long, which were covered with linen cloths.

Harold used to wear clogs down at the cooking place; the sort with a strap over and a clasp. Clogs were better than boots as the floor would get slippery. The floor was concrete and it was cleaned every day after work with soda and boiling water. We had to pay for every drop of water in those days. We had a meter and they used to check it every fortnight.

The Health Inspector, Mr Senior, used to say, 'Y'know Harold, if they were all like you, I wouldn't have a job at all!

A circus parade in Market Street, Colne, around 1910. Worsick's shop is on the right, next to the Golden Boot

You can eat off your cookhouse floor!' Harold used to get the cookhouse whitewashed every month.

When I married, the shop on Market Street used to stay open late at night. We had tables and four lovely forms, scrubbed white. But then the work got to be too much - I also had to do my own washing and housework. When we had finished at the shop, and happen we had sold up, we still had to do all the washing off, and at first we had no hot water. Later I got a gas boiler and had a pipe into my washhouse; I would carry the boiling water into the shop from there.

All the tripe was on little marble shelves and I had nice little plants on the side. I also had an old china horse and a little cart, which I used to put in the middle of the window display with some anemones. A little spastic girl used to come to the shop with her grandma, and if she was naughty her grandma used to tell her that she wouldn't take her past Worsick's to look at the horse and cart! The little girl would say, 'Well, Grandma, it's tekkin' it a long time to walk to t'other end, i'nt it?' When her grandma told me, I would move the horse and cart to the other end. It used to buck the little girl up.

Now every week somebody used to come in a Rolls Royce from Leeds; he was paralysed from the waist. We used to take the tripe out to him on a nice tray with a white serviette. He had a chauffeur, and he'd been ill - nothing would stop on his stomach. We also used to supply Hartley Hospital.

I like tripe, but I never buy it now. I once bought some in the market, and oh!, I couldn't eat it - it just tasted of chloro, same as if they'd bleached it. That put me off and I've never had any since. Cowheel was lovely; I always used to put it in my stew. Harold liked it, and in wintertime it would keep you warm. Lots wouldn't make stew if they couldn't put a little cowheel in it to stiffen it up. Some folk used to put a pig's foot in stew, but there are such a lot of little bones in a pig's foot.

Our tripe was priced at 9d a pound. Well, to take £30 at 9d a time of a Saturday, from eight o'clock till twelve, it wants some working! And Paddy always got a decent wage."

Bradshaw Brothers

Padiham folk are no doubt familiar with the firm of Bradshaw Brothers, which for the past ten years or so has been run by Mr Hayhurst, the present owner. Mr Hayhurst put me in touch with a member of the Bradshaw family, a very active senior citizen. Stanley Bradshaw recounted his story as follows:

"The firm was started in 1895 by my grandfather, who began by boiling offals in a kitchen gas boiler! Later on he bought an old building which had previously been a bakery. He had seven sons and two daughters, all of whom worked in the business at one time or another.

In 1926, at the time of the General Strike, there were three sons running the firm. But trade was quiet and one of them emigrated to Australia. Soon afterwards, at the age of 14, I joined my father, uncle and a cousin. The four of us carried on for several years, supplying about 50 wholesale shops and one retail shop. We had one delivery lorry, and in winter we worked from 7.00am till 5.00pm weekdays, till 1.00pm on Saturday afternoons and for an hour or so on Sunday mornings.

I had to learn all branches of the trade, including picking raw tripes up from the abattoirs, cleaning, boiling and dressing them, as well as the cleaning and de-hairing of cowheels. I also learned about the rendering of tallow and neatsfoot oil. From the age of 18 I delivered to our wholesale and retail outlets, and at times I also worked in the shops themselves.

From 1940 to 1945 I served in the army, whilst my father, uncle and cousin carried on the business. Supplies were difficult to come by and trade slackened off to some extent. Returning home in 1945 I began to plan expansion and after about five years we were serving over 100 shops and five or six market stalls. After Father retired I bought out my uncle and cousin and employed non-family labour. With six people working for me and two delivery lorries, I was confident I could supervise the work and ensure the good quality of the product. To have expanded further would have meant some loss of personal attention and this I was reluctant to do.

The work was hard and the hours long, and on Saturdays - our busiest sales day - we were delivering to six markets and other shops. The markets closed at 6.00pm and then I had to collect empties and returns, which took until about eight or nine o'clock. Our shops didn't close until midnight, and so after collecting from them I seldom got to bed before 1.00am or 2.00am.

On Sunday mornings I had to make another early start, at 7.00am, to collect the bellies from the abattoirs and clean them ready for Monday morning. I had a few hours off on Saturday and Sunday afternoons, but every night I had to visit the works to stoke up our solid fuel boiler and perform other tasks, so it really was a full time job!

I must say I enjoyed the hard work, but I now realise I missed a great deal of family life and I would never do it again. For all that, however, it was a healthy life. During my last

Mrs Lizzie Shuttleworth, Mrs Jeffries and Mrs Worsick in Bell's Yard, behind the Market Street shop, in 1948 five years as a tripedresser I trained up one of my workers to take over, and finally retired at the age of 67.

If there is a decline in tripe eating, I would put it down to the finishing of the cotton industry. In the old days the weavers, coming home from hot, dusty mills, loved their cool, clean tripe for tea. I think there will always be a demand for the product, especially in hot weather as it is so cool and refreshing. And what could be nicer in cold weather than tripe and onions, served piping hot!"

Marsh of Walkden

Mrs Elizabeth Howell (now in her eighties) clearly remembers the period when her mother ran a small tripedressing business in Hodge Road, Walkden.

"At the back of the shop and house was a big boiling shed which we called the cooling shed. There were three coal-fired boilers, two for the bellies, cowheels and trotters, and another small one for fat. There were also two large tanks in which the tripe was cooled, and a long wooden table for dressing and preparing the products for sale.

Grandfather helped with the work whilst Grannie looked after the family. The Co-op slaughterhouse was in Holyoak Road, and it was my job to fetch the offal from there, in a wheelbarrow, assisted by younger siblings.

1876 advertisement

We sometimes bought bellies from a local butcher. Wednesday was the usual boiling day, when Mother was up nearly all night, busy dressing the tripe. I stayed on the sofa in case I was needed, but I invariably fell asleep! It was ready for sale on Thursday, and we had a notice in the window: 'Serving at four'. By eight o'clock that night everything had usually been sold.

There was a stable at the back of the house, where we kept a horse called Fanny and a little trap. Every Thursday morning Grandad went out on deliveries. He used to go down Ellenbrook and past the brickworks over to the 'City' (New Manchester) and I usually went with him. (Ellenbrook Road was called Rosin Lane then.) It was an enjoyable outing, especially in summer, when we sold our own home-made ice-cream as well as tripe.

When the 1914 War came the slaughterhouse was closed and there was a real difficulty in obtaining bellies. Mother had to fight for her rights; she wrote to Mr Clynes (a Manchester MP who became Secretary of the Food Ministry) to ask for help, and was finally allowed to buy six bellies a week, as well as cowheels and trotters. But of these she was obliged to sell one to Mr Billinge, who had a tripe round with a horse and cart." ("Tripe Billinge" had a small shop at Linnyshaw, which was looked after by his wife when he was out on his tripe round.)

"Grandfather, a wheelwright by trade, had to put in some time at the local workhouse, repairing furniture, so he couldn't help out as much. Sometimes I was sent to fetch bellies from Voses in Bolton - 20 to 25 pounds at a time - and one tram driver said to me as I struggled off with the basket, 'Eh lass, you shouldn't be carryin' all that weight!'

Tallow produced from the dressing was sold to a soap-making firm in Liverpool; the bones and hooves went to a glue factory in Pendleton. We stored the tallow in buckets in the coal shed and the few pounds of refined fat was sold in the shop. One day, when the shop was full, Mother had sold all the fat, but one of the customers wouldn't believe her. 'Th'art a liar!' she said. Mother insisted that all she had left was the tallow in the coal shed. 'Fotch it eawt!' the woman commanded. Well, although we had a contract with the soap people, Mam certainly wasn't going to cause a riot over a bucket of tallow. So, as it was full of coal dust, she put the tallow in a pan of boiling water to clean it, and then sold the lot! The soap firm talked of prosecution, but did nothing in the end.

I like tripe when it's still warm from the cooking, but I never ate fat tripe - some wanted all fat. Trotters were sweeter than cowheel; people used to call shin beef and cowheel 'stick-jaw'.

Another tripe shop in Walkden was Simister's on Bolton Road. There was also a shop on Hodge Road; they bought their tripe from Voses, ready dressed."

1922 advertisement

Pendlebury's: the Tripe Colony

I am grateful to Mrs Muriel Graham, grand-daughter of John Pendlebury, the founder of the "Tripe Colony", and to her daughter, Mary Goodier, who willingly told me all they knew of the family.

Around the middle of the nineteenth century John Pendlebury, having received compensation for the loss of his right hand (possibly in a mill accident), started up his own business in the tripe trade. The works was in Simpson Street, Bradford, Manchester, and he also owned a shop on the corner of Forge Lane and Ashton New Road, Bradford, where he sold his products.

Of seven sons and three daughters, only two followed John into the business – his eldest son John Richard *("always known as 'JR' and just as mean!")* and Joseph Henry, born in 1867 and one of the youngest members of the family. Being very much a younger son, Joseph Henry was not in line for a share of the business, and remained merely an employee in the tripe works, first for his father and then for his elder brother. His job involved cleaning out the cows' stomachs and then cooking the tripe ready for sale. It was a gruelling and poorly-paid occupation. In due course he married and fathered nine children; Muriel Graham is the sole surviving member of his family.

Two of Joseph Henry's sons, Harold and Eric, were eventually employed at the works, and Mrs Goodier well remembers being taken to see her uncles there: *"They would come outside to speak to us, and we could feel the heat from inside. There seemed to be clouds of steam everywhere, and they would be pouring with sweat. They worked extremely hard, and if anything arrived to be cooked before they were due to finish they had to stay and do the job, otherwise the offal would go bad – and this was without any overtime pay!*

John Pendlebury was apparently quite an able entrepreneur, for as well as running the tripe works with the help of his eldest son, he also went into the construction business with another of his sons, George William. He boasted that he could build superior houses for the working classes, with bathrooms, at rents that they could afford, in contrast to the usual two-up-two-down type. For their time, these houses were indeed superior, and made from good quality materials such as Accrington brick.

These dwellings "for the working classes" were not available to just anybody; it was said that you had to have a pedigree before you were allowed to go and live on Pendlebury's property! The builders were very particular about their tenants, who were vetted and visited at home. They had to show rent books and had to be clean – and clean-living - people. *"It was one of the most respectable districts in Manchester, and the best-paying district."*

When John retired, his son George William was joined by brother JR in the building venture and they became known as GW & JR Pendlebury, Builders and Contractors.

It has been said that JR's connection with the tripe trade first gave the Tripe Colony its name, but I would contend that it may well have been the involvement with the trade of John Pendlebury himself which was first responsible for the title. It is very likely that the profits from tripedressing gave him the wherewithal to begin building. Whatever the circumstances, the name in no way detracted from the desirability of the dwellings, and they were much sought after.

During the First World War the supply of cattle was restricted and the Pendlebury Brothers, Hills of Ardwick and others in the Manchester area co-operated to help each other. When there was a supply of bellies they shared them out, and thus each

George William Pendlebury, wife Jemima and son Clarence outside their house in North Road, Clayton

firm managed to keep going, if only in a small way. The organisation was called Lancashire Cattle Products, and was a forerunner of the UCP.

The Pendleburys' tripe business evidently did well; they owned several shops in such areas as Hulme, Ardwick, Miles Platting and Harpurhey, and supplied other shops and butchers with their products. JR, as one of the founders of the UCP, was also a director of that concern, whereas John Henry continued working under him as a mere dresser, or "boiling man", as Mrs Graham calls him.

Today, the tripe works and all the area around Simpson Street has been demolished. Building on the Tripe Colony was curtailed when Lloyd George introduced his "Form Four Act" which, according to the two brothers, made it unprofitable for them to carry on. So JR and George William decided to close down, sold all the plant and divided up the properties. In time these passed to their respective sons, Norman and Clarence, who then became co-owners of the Colony.

In the 1970s, due to a number of factors, the houses were sold, some to Manchester Corporation and some to a private developer. The Tripe Colony still stands, with most of the houses modernised and improved. There is, however, no longer any connection with the Pendlebury family – or with tripe!

* * * * *

Mr Reid of Stockport remembers that in the 1920s the biggest tripedressing factory in the town was in Pool Lane. Here, the raw tripe *("a horrible green colour")* was washed and treated with chemicals to whiten it. *"It was the sort of place that was looked at with awe by local children."*

Another tripe works, in Back Water Street, was regularly used as a boxing booth at the weekend!

Mr Reid recalls how his grandmother used to give him honeycomb tripe and elder, garnished with black pepper and vinegar, topped with a tomato and pickled onion; this was accompanied by brown bread, bought specially. Trotters were eaten as takeaway meals, and often consumed at the pictures, music-halls and theatres. Boiled cowheel or meat and cowheel pie was regarded as being more of a luxury. Families would have tripe two or three times a week on average, and it was certainly the commonest meal of the nineteen-twenties and thirties.

Outside Pendlebury's tripe works. Joseph Henry Pendlebury, brother of "JR", is third from right. George William Pendlebury is also in the group

Lancashire Tripedressers and Dealers, 1924

ABBOTT Richard, 90 King Street, Blackburn
ADAMS George, 64 Chester Road, Hulme, M/c
ADAMS J E, 179 Egerton Street, Farnworth
AINLEY A, 112 Lower Broughton Rd, Salford
AINSWORTH John, 151 Bolton Road, Blackburn
ALDRED Thomas, 157 Chapel Street, Leigh
ALLAN A, 97 Picton Rd, Wavertree, Liverpool
ALLEN Bros, Warrington New Road, St Helens
ALLEN & Co Ltd, 76,77 St Johns Mkt, L'pool
ALLEN Joseph W, 130 Westfield St, St Helens
ALMOND Wm Ltd, 163 Penny St; 6 Jubilee St & 32 Whalley Range; works, George St W, Blackburn; 10 Coronation St & 119 Talbot Rd, Blackpool; 4 Cheapside & Moor Brook St,Preston; 28 Horsemarket St; 59 Winwick St & 22 Darlington St, Wigan; 45 Orford Lane & Lilford Street, Warrington
ALMOND William, 28 New Bank Road, Blackburn
ALMOND W, 51 Warbreck Road, Blackpool
ARMSTRONG J, 33 Garnett St, Hightown, M/cr
ARNOLD & HOUGH Ltd, Arnold St; 126 Cavendish St; 100,101 Market Hall; 203a & 287d Stamford St; 43 Katherine St; 52 & 286 Stockport Rd; 31 Warrington St & 76 Stamford Sq, Ashton-u-Lyne; 15 Henshaw St; 150 Manchester St & 19 Yorkshire St, Oldham & 104 High Street & 43 Market Street, Stalybridge
ARNOLD Samuel, 278 Ordsall Lane, Salford
ASHTON B, 52 Market Street, Shaw, Oldham
ASHTON Charles, 1 Peter Street, Altrincham
ASHTON James, 20 Market St, Blackley, M/c
ASHWORTH William, 162 Dumers La, Radcliffe
ASPINAL James Henry, 29 Derby St, Salford
ASPINALL R, 120 Market St, Hindley, Wigan
ASPINALL S, 106 Adswood Road, Stockport
ASTIN Ebenezer, 8 Burnley Road, Padiham
ASTIN H, 105 Gisburn Rd, Barrowford, Nelson
ASTLEY T, 36 Barnes St, Clayton-le-Moors
ASTON B&N, 520 Oldham Rd, Newton Heath, M/c
ATHERTON R, 2 Corporation St, Stalybridge
ATHERTON W, 91 Talbot Road, Blackpool
ATKINSON J, 85 St Helens Road, Bolton

BAILEY F, 68 Bradley Hall Road, Nelson
BAINES Mrs Alice Ann, 117 Darwen St, B'burn
BAINES C, 45 Whalley Road, Accrington
BAINES Robert S, 26 New Market St, B'burn
BAINES W, 2 Croft St & 368 Bolton Rd,Darwen
BAIRSTOW S, 52 Padiham Road, Burnley
BALL John, 7 Rochdale Road, Shaw, Oldham
BANKS E A, 225 Oldham Road, Rochdale
BANKS J, 100 Winter Hey Lane, Horwich
BANKS J W, 115 Brackley Street, Farnworth
BARKER Fred, 18 Union Square, Bury
BARLOW M, 197 Albert Road, Farnworth
BARLOW Mrs Mary, 30 Weaste Road, Salford
BARNARD G, 106 Whalley Range, Blackburn
BARNES J, 763 Oldham Rd, Bardsley, A-u-L
BARNES William, 564 Oldham Rd, Failsworth
BARRATT Mrs E, 314 Hyde Rd, Ardwick, M/c

BARROW MASTER BUTCHERS' ASSOCIATION, 58 Cavendish St & 109 Dalton Rd, Barrow
BATES Samuel, 170 Langworthy Road, Salford
BATLEY Mrs Emily, 54 Renshaw St, Hulme, M/c
BATTY Tom, 115 Darley Street, Bolton
BATTYE Albert, 35 Rusholme Rd, C-on-M, M/c
BAXENDALE James, Pump Street, Blackburn
BELL Mrs J, 41 Wilmslow Rd, Rusholme, M/c
BENNETT Mrs Ellen, 300 Rochdale Road, M/c
BENNION M A, 1010 Ashton Old Road, Openshaw
BENT A, 157 Love La, Heaton Norris, Stockpt
BENTLEY Miss A, 13 Furthergate, Blackburn
BERRY James, 123 Chorley Road, Swinton
BERRY W H, 1 Beardwood Rd, Blackley, M/c
BERTENSHAW J, 261 Queen St, Hurst, A-u-L
BIBBY James, 147 Greengate, Salford
BISSETT Donald & Sons, 164a Boundary St & 46 Fox Street, Liverpool
BLACKBURN Wm, 158 Chapel House Rd, Nelson
BLACKTOP A, 242 Conran St, Harpurhey, M/c
BLORE John, Ripponden Road, Oldham
BOARDMAN James, 18 Bury Street, Radcliffe
BOLTON HIDE, SKIN & FAT CO LTD, 31 Market Hall & 46 Standishgate, Wigan
BOND J C, 87a Lytham Rd, S Shore, B'pool
BOOTH T H, 207 Lower Broughton St, Salford
BOOTH W, 227 Oldham Rd, Longsight, Oldham
BOSTOCK Samuel, 128 Daw Bank & 9 Millgate, Stockport
BOSTOCK W H, 587 Gorton Rd, Reddish, Stkpt
BOWN G H, 216 Guide Lane, Audenshaw, M/c
BOYD J W, 22 Blackburn Street, Radcliffe
BRADBURY Wm, 42 Clifton Street, Lytham
BRADDOCK Mrs E, 45 Upper Moss La, Hulme,M/c
BRADLEY F, 86 Broughton Rd, Pendleton
BRADLEY H, 134 Darwen St, Blackburn
BRADSHAW Alfred, 74 Bedford St, Hulme, M/c
BRADSHAW BROS, 13 Church St & 65 Burnley Rd Padiham, Burnley
BRADSHAW J R, 55 Plantation St, Accrington
BRADSHAW Mrs Mary, 17 Tulketh Brow, Preston
BREDBURY John Ltd, 85 Oldham Rd & 167 Stamford Street, Ashton-under-Lyne
BREELEY Mrs Annie, 524 Rochdale Road, M/c
BRENNAN Mrs C, 94 Queen St, Great Harwood
BRIDGE Fred, 676 Rochdale Rd, Manchester
BRIDGE R, 273 Bacup Rd, Cloughfold, M/c
BRIDGES Thos, 355 Rochdale Rd, Bacup
BRIGGS A & Son, 452 Oldham Rd, Ardwick, M/c
BRIGGS B, 128 Bury Old Rd, Besses o'th'Barn
BRIGGS F, 47 Church St, Newton Heath, M/c
BRIGGS F, 126 Droylsden Rd, Newton Heath
BRINDLE John, 290 North Road, Preston
BRINDLE W, 40 Dill Hall Lane, Church
BROADBENT G H, 360 Middleton Road, Oldham
BROADY J, 228 Ashton New Rd, Beswick, M/c
BROMILEY James, 50 Steeley Lane, Chorley
BROOKS Mrs Ann Ellen, Whalley Banks, B'burn
BROOKS Harry, 11 Stockport Rd, Denton, M/c
BROOKS W, 78 Walthew La, Platt Br, Wigan

BROUGHTON & CO, 24 Market St, Warrington
BROUGHTON Mrs M A, 288 Wigan Road, Bolton
BROW Wm, 31 Charnley St, Mill Hill, B'burn
BROWN, Mrs A, 95 Tonge Moor Road, Bolton
BROWN G H, 57 M/c Rd, Heaton Norris, Stkpt
BROWN Mrs M, 166 Conran St, Harpurhey, M/C
BROWN M E, 225 Wellington St, Bradford, M/c
BROWN R H, 61 Liverpool Road, Eccles
BROWN Thos, 87 Market St, Stalybridge
BROWN Wm, 14 Broadstone Road, Reddish
BROWN Wm James, 58 Thirlmere Rd, Liverpool
BUCKLEY Harry, 87 Thompson La, Hollinwood
BUCKLEY Samuel, 15 Stockport Rd, Denton, M/c
BULLCOCK Mrs E, 76 Blackburn Rd, Accrington
BUNN Mrs V, 154 Garforth St, Oldham
BURNS Mrs Ada, 3 Fold Street, Moston, M/c
BUSH Mrs N, 620 Ashton Old Rd, Openshaw, M/C
BUTTERWORTH E, 50 Rochdale Lane, Heywood
BYRNE R Ltd, Prospect House, Albert St, Mill
    Hill & Ainsworth Street, Blackburn

CALLOGHAN P, 87 Gt Portwood St, Stockport
CALVERT Mrs J, 93 Lees Road, Oldham
CARR Mrs Emma, 210 Fairfield Road, Droylsden
CARRADINE Mrs M, 162 Moston Lane, Moston
CARTER Mrs Sarah, 67 Tamworth Street, Hulme
CASE Mrs E A, 22 Winter Hey Lane, Horwich
CAWLEY Frances, 85b Manchester Rd, Ardwick
CAYLEY V, 19 Burnley Rd, Brierfield, Burnley
CHADBOND G H, 98 Market St, Farnworth
CHADWICK A, 5 Whitefield St, Hapton, Burnley
CHADWICK Mrs S M, 140 Railway St, Nelson
CHAPMAN John, 17 Taylor's Road, Stretford
CHEADLE Richard, 5b Bolton Rd, Farnworth
CHEETHAM Mrs G, 87a Church Street, Eccles
CHESTER C, 13 King St West, Stockport
CHRISTIAN Miss E, 448 Mill St, Liverpool
CLAPHAM Mrs S E, 392 Lees Road, Oldham
CLARK Ernest, 22 Stanley Street, Bury
CLARKE Mrs M, 177 Egerton Street, Oldham
CLARKE Mrs M, 12 Whittaker La, Heaton Park
CLARKE Philip, 27 Market Street, Droylsden
CLAYTON Robert, 27 Church Street, Fleetwood
CLEGG Abraham L, Abel Street, Burnley
CLEMINSON S, 5 Griffin St, Witton, B'burn
CLEWORTH Robert, 87 Castle St, Tyldesley
CLORAN T, 27 Radcliffe Rd, Royton, Oldham
CLOUGH J, 294 Tottington Rd, Woolfold, Bury
CLOUGH Mrs M A, 158 Blackburn Road, Bolton
CLOWES G, 497 Manchester Road, Hollinwood
COCHRANE J H, 401 Eccles New Road, Salford
COCKER William, 163 Padiham Road, Burnley
COLBY Mrs M J, 219 City Road, Hulme
COLE John, 51 Lostock Street, Manchester
COLLINS Mrs M, 3 Liverpool Road, St Helens
COLLISON F, 109 Buxton Road, Stockport
CONNOLLEY Mrs M, 204 Greengate, Salford
COOPER A, Arch St; 22 Yorkshire Street, 80
    Briercliffe Rd; 76 Parliament St; 137
    Westgate; 6 Market St; 214 Colne Rd; 54
    Abel St & 189 St James St, Burnley & 5
    Moor Lane, Padiham, Burnley
COOPER W J, 551 Blackburn Rd, Darwen
COPPOCK W, 66 Montague Street, Blackburn
COUSINS Mrs M, 92 Broad Street, Pendleton
COWELL Henry, 41 Newchurch Rd, Rawtenstall
COX John (Bury) Ltd, 14 King St; 28 Hay-
    market St; 129 Rochdale Rd; 2a Wash La;
    37 Walmersley Rd; 23 Princess Street; 64
    Bolton Rd; 14 Parkhills Rd & 140 Bolton
    St, Bury; 65 Blackburn St, Radcliffe, and
    36 Eastbank Street, Southport
COX John, 455 Bury New Road, Pendleton
COX John William, 4 Market Place, Colne
CRANGLE Mrs J, 270 Fylde Road, Preston
CRANSHAW W & Co, 62&64 Ribbleton La, Preston
CRANSHAW Wm, 3 Ormskirk Road, Preston
CRANSTON W & Co, 25 Fylde St & 155 Friar-
    gate, Preston
CRAWSHAW H 133 Sandygate, Burnley
CRERAR James, 141 Alexandra Rd, Moss Side
CRITCHLEY Mrs M, 382 Stretford Road, Hulme
CROFT George, 12 Ellesmere Street, Leigh
CROFT J S, 113 Atherton Rd, Hindley, Wigan
CROFT J K, 64 Darlington Street, Wigan
CROOK C, 89 Chorlton Rd, Brooks's Bar, M/cr
CROOK Joseph, 85 Whit Lane, Pendleton
CROSSLEY Frank, 38 King Street, Southport
CROSSLEY John, 75 Halifax Road, Rochdale
CROWTHER J, 31 Featherstall Rd N, Oldham
CUNLIFFE J, 33 Maudland Bank, Preston

DALY Mrs E B, 324 Liverpool Street, Salford
DARDIS John, 101 Olive Lane, Darwen
DAVIES Alfred, 29 Cairo Street, Warrington
DAVIES John, 203 Curzon Rd, Hurst, A-u-L
DAVIES S 677 Chorley Old Road, Bolton
DAVIS R 75 Middle Hillgate, Stockport
DAWSON E, 138 Oldham Rd, Miles Platting
DEAN E, 1 King Edward Ter, Barrowford, Nelson
DEAN Philip, 37 Church Street, Colne
DEARDEN A, 221 Manchester Road, Kearsley
DEARDEN Esau, 54 Chesham Road, Bury
DERBY A, 119 Barlow Moor Rd & 78 Wilbraham
    Road, Chorlton-cum-Hardy, Manchester
DEWHIRST Mrs C, 79 Hr Hillgate, Stockport

DICKENS C, 1322 Ashton Old Road, Openshaw
DICKSON Mrs D, 24 Covered Market, St Helens
DICKSON P, 68 Waterloo Street, St Helens
DITCHFIELD Samuel, 18 Regent Road, Salford
DIXON P, 24 Covered Market, St Helens
DOBSON J H, 58 Queen St, Gt Harwood, B'burn
DODD Mrs E, 14 Union St, Tranmere, L'pool
DOLMAN L, 77 Upr Conran St, Harpurhey, M/cr
DONALDSON James, 71 Scholes, Wigan
DONE Richard, 2 Enys Street, Pendleton
DOWD Charles, 98a Durham Street, Rochdale
DOYLE George, 813 Rochdale Rd, Manchester
DUCKWORTH J, 55 Penny Street, Lancaster
DUCKWORTH J W, 20 Salford, Clitheroe
DUCKWORTH Joe, 65 Euston Rd & 54 Yorkshire
    Street, Morecambe
DUCKWORTH J, 6 Church Street, Lancaster
DUXBURY John, 310 Bolton Rd, Blackburn
DUXBURY O, 40 Sudell Side Street, Darwen
DUXBURY Thomas, 419 Halliwell Road, Bolton
DYSON Mrs J, 128 West Park Street, Salford
DYSON Watson (Branch of UCP), 24 Market Pl
    and branches, 3 Hilton St; 138 Gt Ancoats
    St; 4 Peter St; 363 Ashton New Rd, Brad-
    ford and Howarth St, Bradford; 1145 & 1262
    Ashton Old Rd, Openshaw; 103 & 660 Stock-
    port Rd, Ardwick & 16 Alexandra Rd, Moss
    Side, Manchester

EASTHAM T, 88 Scotland Rd, Blackburn
ECKERSALL J, 440 Bury New Road, Pendleton
EDGE Mrs Annie, 148 Lwr Moss La, Hulme, M/c
EDGERTON S, 29 Radclyffe Street, Oldham
EDWARDS W, 5 Market St, Hindley, Wigan
ELSON John, 74 Huddersfield Road, Oldham
ENTWISTLE R, 49 Wellington St; 107 Warring-
    ton St & 103 Market Hall, Ashton-u-Lyne
ENTWISTLE W, 124 Gisburn Rd, Barrowford,
    Nelson
ETCHELLS J J, 7 Prince's Street, Stockport
EVANS Mrs M, 262 Halliwell Rd, Bolton
EVANS S, 10 Lees Rd, Mossley, Manchester
EYERS J E, 431 Ashton Old Rd, Openshaw, M/c

FAGGIANA Mrs L, 140 London Road, Manchester
FAIRCLOUGH W, 151 Marsh Lane, Preston
FARRAND S, 467 Huddersfield Rd, Stalybridge
FARRAR Bros, 18a Burnley Rd, Todmorden
FARRELL P H, 89 High Street, Little Lever
FARRINGTON T, 119 Love Lane, Heaton Norris
FARROW C, Hr Market St, Kearsley, Farnworth
FAWCETT W C, 92 Napier St E, Werneth, Oldham
FAWKES Mrs E, 401 Edge La, Droylsden, M/cr
FIELDEN L, 105 Oxford Road, Burnley
FIELDING Fred, 138 Peel Street, Farnworth
FIELDING John, 301 Liverpool Rd, Patricroft

FILDES Mrs E, 71 College Street, St Helens
FIRTH Mrs Jane, 37a Church Street, Eccles
FISH Mrs E, 76a Raikes Road, Blackpool
FISHER Wm, 157 Higher Hillgate, Stockport
FLAHERTY J, 18 Naylor St, Oldham Rd, M/cr
FLETCHER Mrs S, 310 Chorley Old Rd, Bolton
FLETCHER W, 9 Barlow Moor Rd, Didsbury, M/c
FLINT C, 519 Huddersfield Road, Oldham
FLINTOFF Mrs M, 288 Ribbleton Lane, Preston
FLITCROFT Jesse, 292 Bury Road, Bolton
FLOOD Miss Annie, 2 St Simon St, Salford
FORREST W H, 211 Lancaster Rd, Preston
FORRESTER M, 106 Claremont Rd, Moss Side
FOSTER E, 12 Oldham Rd, Springhead, Oldham
FOSTER J, 33 Walthew La, Platt Br, Wigan
FOSTER T W, 115 Blackburn Rd, Gt Harwood,
    Blackburn
FRANCIS G, 171 Manchester Rd, Broadheath,
    Altrincham

GALLAGHER J, 6 Hermitage St, Rishton, B'Burn
GARLICK Ernest, 40 Levens Street, Pendleton
GARNER Henry, 231 Broad Street, Pendleton
GARRAWAY E, 268 Gorton La, West Gorton, M/c
GARSIDE Charles, 35 Glodwick, Oldham
GARVEY Mrs M, 349 Ainsworth Rd, Radcliffe
GAUGER J, 11 Upper Brook Street, Ulverston
GEE E, 597 Burnley Rd, Crawshaw Booth
GEE Mrs J, 266 Chorley Moor Rd, Horwich
GERRARD G, 426 Tyldesley Rd, Hindsford
GIBSON J, 98 Ormskirk Rd, Pemberton, Wigan
GLEAVE Mrs M, Heyes Lane, Alderley Edge
GOODYEAR Mrs A, 28 Clarendon St, Hulme, M/c
GOSLING Mrs A, 3 Walton Rd, Stockton Heath
GOUGH Mrs L, 33 Cross St, Ashton-on-Mersey
GRAHAM Edward, 42&44 Oriel St, Liverpool
GRAHAM E, 71 St John's Market, Liverpool
GRAHAM J A, 57 Whit Lane, Pendleton
GRANGE Mrs E, 286 Queens Rd, Miles Platting
GREENHALGH Mrs A, 8 King Edward's Buildings,
    Bury Old Rd, Cheetham Hill, Manchester
GREENHALGH James, 219 Deane Road, Bolton
GREENHALGH P, 471 Blackburn Road, Bolton
GREENHALGH Wm, 270 Hollins Lane, Hollins
GREENWOOD A, 204 Ashton New Rd, Beswick, M/c
GREGORY Fred, 11 George Street, Oldham
GRIFFITHS Arthur, 8 Stanley St, Southport
GRIFFITHS W A, 110 Liverpool Rd, Patricroft
GRIMSHAW Mrs B, 114 Frog Lane, Wigan
GRIMSHAW T A, 173 Butler St, Oldham Rd, M/c
GRIMSHAW W, 459 Whalley New Road, Blackburn
GRUNDY A, 13&15 Burnley Road, Colne

HACKER Mrs S, 493 Eccles New Road, Salford
HACKING E, 102 Audley Range, Blackburn

Broad Street, Salford, in 1970. A former Hill & Hiley tripe shop not long before demolition

HACKING M, 257 Featherstall Rd N, Oldham
HACKING Mrs R, 8 Whalley Old Rd, Blackburn
HACKNEY John, 175 Bell Lane, Bury
HALE Mrs E, 107 Northenden Rd, Sale
HALKYARD R, 122 Rochdale Road, Oldham
HALL H, 74 Two Trees La, Denton, Manchester
HALL James, 76 High Street, Lees, Oldham
HALL W, 73 Milnrow Rd, E Crompton, Oldham
HALLEY J, 3 Hough La, Lwr Broughton, Salford
HALLIWELL Fred, 386 Claremont Rd, Rusholme
HALLIWELL G, 26 Booth St, Ashton-under-Lyne
HAMBLETON Mrs E, 274 Tatton Street, Salford
HAMER F, 303 Blackburn Road, Bolton
HAMILTON Mrs E, 38 Middleton Road, Royton
HAMMOND Mrs M, 62 Furthergate, Blackburn
HAMPSON Miss A, 155 Ainsworth Rd, Radcliffe
HANBY J A, 58 Islington, Liverpool
HAND W H, 211 New Bridge La, Stockport
HANKINSON Mrs C, 41 Chapel St, Pendleton
HARGREAVES G, 138 Scotland Rd, Nelson
HARGREAVES H, 39 Queen St, Great Harwood
HARGREAVES W, 285 Blackburn Rd, Accrington
HARRISON Miss A, 33 Burnley Rd, Accrington
HARTIGAN Mrs S, 245 Oldham Road, Manchester
HARTLEY T, Bacup Road, Waterfoot
HARTLEY Miss S M, 215 Hyde Road, W Gorton
HARWOOD Mrs M, 100 Wellington St, Gorton
HASLAM J, 68 Manchester Rd W, Little Hulton
HASLAM R, 85 Bridgeman Street, Bolton
HAUGHEY T, 195 Tipping St, Ardwick, M/cr
HAWORTH Mrs E, 198 Audley Range, Blackburn
HAWORTH J, 103 Roegreave Rd, Oswaldtwistle
HAYES M, 21 New Chapel St, Mill Hill, B'brn
HAYES Mrs M D, 10 Breck St, Poulton-le-Fylde
HAYNES T, 42 Rochdale Rd, Harpurhey, M/cr
HEATH T, 6 Elephant Street, Accrington
HEATON Robert, 175 Edge La, Droylsden, M/cr
HENDERSON G, 434 Gorton Road, Reddish
HETHERINGTON J, 68 Market St, Ulverston
HETHERINGTON J, 179 Great Moor St, Bolton
HEWITT J H, 24 Brinksway, Stockport
HEYS James, Fish Market, Darwen
HEYS J B, 35 Parker Lane, Burnley
HEYWOOD P, 30 St Stephen Street, Salford
HICKS A, 484 Cheetham Hill Rd, Manchester
HIGGINS Tom, 17 High Street, Stalybridge
HIGGINSON John, 39 Broadstone Road, Reddish
HIGGINSON Miss S J, 281 Oldham Rd, Rochdale
HIGHAM R, 834 Hollins Road, Hollinwood
HILEY A&G, Chaney Street & 193 Broad Street
   Pendleton
HILEY Beaumont, 132 Church Street, Eccles
HILL Mrs Amelia , 2 Cook Street, Pendleton
HILL Mrs W E E, 215 Hodge Lane, Salford
HILL F (wholesale) office & works, Rennie
   St, Salford; and retail, 208 Regent Rd,
   Salford, and 158 & 209 Stretford Road,
   Hulme, Manchester
HILL J S (wholesale) (branch of UCP Ltd);
   abattoirs, Green St, Ladybarn. 125 Mar-
   ket St; 98 Oldham Rd, Miles Platting;
   780 Ashton Old Rd; 69 Chancery La and
   153 & 155 Brunswick St, Ardwick; 29
   Oxford Rd, C-on-M and 80 Preston Street,
   Hulme, Manchester. 56 Castle St,Edgeley,
   Stockport
HILTON A, 314 Rochdale Road, Oldham
HILTON James, 5 Broadway Street, Oldham
HILTON Jonathan, 89 Ellor Street, Salford
HODCROFT Mrs M, 35 King St, Stretford, M/cr
HODGES A, 97 Parliament Street, Burnley
HOLDEN T&J, 268 Newcnurch Rd, Stacksteads
HOLDEN J T, 165 Blackburn Road, Darwen
HOLDEN J D, 19 High St, Shaw, Oldham
HOLDEN Mrs M, 477 Mill St, Bradford, M/cr
HOLDEN Mrs E, 142 Whalley Old Rd, B'burn
HOLDING Mrs E, 189 City Road, Hulme, M/cr
HOLDSWORTH J, 13a Primet Hill, Colne
HOLLAND A, 3 Yorkshire St; 19b Oxford Rd &
   164 Gannow Lane, Burnley
HOLLAND James, 19a Tunnel Street, Burnley
HOLLINS Percy, 89 High Street, Stalybridge
HOLLIS G, 433 Manchester Rd, Hollinwood
HOLT William, 340 Oldham Rd, Newton Heath
HOPE Thomas, 152 Cross Lane, Salford
HORROCKS A, 110 Buttermarket St, Warrington
HORROCKS S, 467 Halliwell Road, Bolton
HOUGH G, 133 Tipping Street, Ardwick, M/cr
HOUGHTON Miss E, 242 Hyde Rd, West Gorton
HOWARD J, 196 Haslingden Rd, Rawtenstall
HOWARD Miss J, 115 Moston La, Barnes Gn,M/c
HOWARD Mrs S, 40 George St, Altrincham
HOWARTH A, 43 Sandygate, Burnley
HOWARTH Mrs E A, 57 Meadow St, Preston
HOWARTH James, 78 Green Road, Colne
HOWARTH J W, 299 Halifax Road, Rochdale
HOWARTH Samuel, 354 Shaw Road, Oldham
HOWCROFT Miss M A, 36 St Helens Rd, Bolton
HOWSON Levi, 32 Covered Market, St Helens
HOYLE Thomas, 1 Union Street, Ardwick, M/cr
HUGHES Fred, 33 York Street, Wigan
HUGHES J, 30 Henrietta St, Ashton-u-Lyne
HULL H F, 6 Ashton Street, Preston
HULLEY E, 602 Lees Road, Oldham
HULME Joshua, 40 Seymour St, Denton, M/cr

HULME J & Sons, 199 Ashton Rd & 2 Manchester
   Road, Denton, Manchester
HULME J & Sons, 171 King St & 38b Union St,
   Oldham
HULME J jun, 262 Katherine St, Ashton-u-L
HULME J, 132 Stoneclough Rd, nr Kearsley
HULME R H, 16 Railway Street, Altrincham
HULME W, 293 Manchester Rd, Hollinwood, and
   344 Manchester Street, Oldham
HUNSLEY C, 24 Lansdowne Rd, Crumpsall, M/c
HUNT T & Son, 83 Victoria Road, Widnes
HUNT Mrs M, 104 Church Street, Preston
HUNTER Jas, 238 Halliwell Rd, Bolton
HURST Mrs M A, 62 N Porter St, Manchester
HUTCHINSON & STRACHAN, 69 Melbourne Street,
   Stalybridge
HUTCHINSON J, 143 High Street, Stalybridge
HYDE Mrs A, 48 Bolton Road, Walkden

IDDON John, 1 Market Street, Little Lever
INCE Mrs J, 26 Dean La, Newton Heath, M/cr
INGHAM Mrs A, 21 Wood Street, Middleton
INGHAM J & Sons, 106 St John's Mkt, L'pool
IRELAND Miss A, 48 Richmond St, Accrington
IRLAM A, 194 Bolton Rd, Irlams o'th'Height
IRLAM Samuel, Travis Street, Pendleton
IRLAM Samuel Ltd. 3 Toad La; 65 Spotland
   Rd; 59 Milkstone Rd; 66 Whitworth Rd;
   145 Yorkshire St; 10 & 64 Drake St; Hal-
   ifax Rd & Primrose St, Rochdale; 742 &
   838 Manchester Rd, Castleton; 19 High
   St; 5 Barker St; 58 Bottom o'th'Moor &
   4 & 290 Manchester St, Oldham; 121 Miln-
   row Rd, Rochdale; 12 Rochdale Rd,Royton;
   5 Milnrow Rd, East Crompton, & 19 Church
   Street, Littleborough
IRLAM Samuel, 24 Merefield St, Rochdale
IRLAMS Samuel, 26 Long St & 39 Manchester
   New Road, Middleton
ISHERWOOD R, 94 Water Street, Radcliffe
ISHERWOOD Mrs S, 41 King Street, Leigh

JACKSON E, 24 York St, Edgeley, Stockport
JACKSON H, 93 Clowes Street, West Gorton
JACKSON J T, 197 London Road, Hazel Grove
JACKSON Mrs S, 22 Liverpool Street, Salford
JAMES William, 3 Pink Street, Blackburn
JEFFERS Mrs Catherine, 693 Rochdale Rd &
   (wholesale) Warford St, Dantzic St, M/c
JEPSON Edgar, 113 Ashton Old Road, Ardwick
JEPSON J Ltd, Fish Market, Darwen
JEPSON John, Market Arcade, Darwen
JEPSON W R, 211 Duckworth Street, Darwen
JERVIS J, 57 Gt Clowes St, Lower Broughton
JERVIS W I, Reedsholme, Burnley Road,
   Rawtenstall
JOHNSON Alfred, 126 Scholes, Wigan
JOHNSON Miss M A, 9 Nicholas St, Lancaster
JOHNSON T, 26 Castle St, Edgeley, Stockport
JOHNSON W, 104 Friargate, Preston
JOLLEY F, 88 Fairfield Road, Droylsden, M/c
JOLLEY F, 252 Oldham Rd, Newton Heath, M/c
JONES H, 274 Lees Road, Oldham
JONES S, 183 Elliott Street, Tyldesley
JONES C H, 623 Stockport Rd, Longsight, M/c
JONES M, 31 Moston Lane, Barnes Green, M/c
JONES S, 802 Ashton New Rd, Clayton, M/c
JONES William, 103 City Road, Hulme, M/c
JUDGE Mrs M A, 48 Stockbridge Rd, Padiham

KAY Ralph & Sons, 13 Church St & 89 Market
   St, Atherton
KAY Arthur, 122 Bradshawgate & 23a Chapel
   Street, Leigh
KAY Fred, 1 Bell Lane, Bury
KAY H, 47 Castle Street, Tyldesley
KAY Mrs S, 2 Horsedge Street, Oldham
KELLY Robert, 96 Hall Street, Moston, M/c
KEMBLE R, 42 Yew Tree Rd, Rusholme, M/c
KEMP W, 54 Higher Hillgate, Stockport
KENT & SWARBRICK LTD, 15 St Petersgate; 7
   Tiviot Dale; 134 Princes St; 246 Heaton
   La, Heaton Mersey & works, 27 Water St,
   Portwood, Stockport
KENYON H, 1 Market St, Royton, Oldham
KENYON H, 33 Stand Lane, Radcliffe
KENYON J, 127 Lightbowne Road, Moston, M/c
KENYON W, 73 Middleton Rd, Royton, Oldham
KERSHAW M A, 903 Ashton Old Rd, Openshaw
KING P J, 29 Eccles New Road, Salford
KINGHAM, M J, 275 Abbey Hey La, Gorton, M/c
KINSEY J, 47 Butler Street, Oldham Rd, M/c
KIRBY Mrs M, 73 Tatton Street, Salford
KIRBY Robert, 28 Renshaw St, Gorton, M/c
KIRBY Thomas, 78 Oxford Rd, Burnley
KIRKHAM Mrs M, 56 Walmer St, Rusholme, M/c
KNIGHT W H, 158 Whalley Rd, Clayton-le-Moors
KNOWLES W, Stockbridge Road, Padiham
KNOWLSON A, 235 Ashton New Rd, Beswick, M/c

LABIN T, 99 Bolton Street, Chorley
LAMBERT A, 522 Liverpool Rd, Patricroft
LAMPTON E, 111 Every Street, Ancoats, M/c
LANGHORN A, Porter St, Werneth, Oldham
LANGTREE J, 58 Trafalgar Street, Burnley
LANSDALE Miss H, 8 Arlington St, Salford

LAPWORTH Mrs M, 35 Tatton Street, Salford
LAW F, 19 Blackburn Rd, Great Harwood
LAW J R, 51 Central Drive, Blackpool
LAW Wm, Bamber Bridge, Preston
LAWTON Mrs E, 7 Astley Gate, Blackburn
LEACH Abel, Market St, Whitworth, Rochdale
LEACH Chas, 24 Shaw Heath, Stockport
LEACH G, 221 Entwistle Rd, Rochdale
LEATHER Wm, 85 Wigan Lane, Wigan
LEE James, 76 St Helens Road, Bolton
LEE John J, 40 Gloucester Street, Salford
LEE Mrs K, 117 Ashton New Rd, Beswick, M/c
LEES Evan, 238 Drake Street, Rochdale
LEES J H, 41 Whit Lane, Pendleton
LEES Joseph, 351 Halliwell Road, Bolton
LEONARD F C, 35 Pool St, Poolstock, Wigan
LEONARD Mrs S J, 167 Marsh Lane, Preston
LEVER R, 841 Briercliffe Rd, Burnley
LILLY John, 219 Elliott Street, Tyldesley
LISTER E, 183 Huddersfield Rd, Oldham
LISTER Edward, 50 Abbey Hills Road, Oldham
LIVESEY R, 329 Washbrook, Hollinwood,Oldham
LIVESEYS 178 Rochdale Road, Royton, Oldham
LIVSEY Angelo, 143 Oldham Rd & 178 Rochdale
   Road, Royton, Oldham
LLOYD Mrs, 15a Market Street, Bacup
LOFTAS W, 18 Seymour Gro, Old Trafford, M/c
LOMAX G, 118 Heaton St, Denton, Manchester
LONGWORTH J, 74 Egerton Street, Farnworth
LORD J T, 60 Market Street, Westhoughton
LORD S E, 5 Hardman Lane, Failsworth
LOWE Mrs A A, 23 Cross Lane, Salford
LOWNDES Albert, 124 Stockport Rd, Longsight
LUMB J, 15 Waterloo Road, Blackpool
LYLES Mrs G, 73 High St, Newton-le-Willows
LYNCH James, 22 Bank Top, Blackburn

McBRIDE M, 16a Tudor Sq, Dalton-in-Furness
McLAUGHLIN T W, 70 St John's Market, L'pool
McMANUS C, 354 Mill Street, Bradford, M/cr
MARLOW E, 54 Cross St, Gorton, Manchester
MARLOW L, 679 Ashton Old Rd, Bradford, M/cr
MARSH S, 58 Hodge Rd, Walkden, Manchester
MARSHALL E, 116 Bridge Street, Heywood
MARTIN J&J, 121 Albert Rd & Market Place,
   Farnworth
MARTINDALE J, 173 Chorley Old Road, Bolton
MASON E, 718 Oldham Rd, Newton Heath, M/cr
MASON H K, 109b Manchester Road, Swinton

Pendlebury's tripe shop on Oldham Street, Manchester

The Bolton Tripe Map *(1911)*

1	Percy G Unsworth	498 Blackburn Road
2	Jonathan Isherwood	472 Blackburn Road
3	Vose & Son	464 Blackburn Road
4	William Singleton	303 Blackburn Road
5	Samuel Horrocks	467 Halliwell Road
6	Charles Clough	158 Blackburn Road
7	William Downward	351 Halliwell Road
8	John Baxter	126 Blackburn Road
9	Abraham Evans	262 Halliwell Road
10	George Adamson	81 Blackburn Road
11	John L Mason	238 Halliwell Road
12	Abraham Evans	41 Blackburn Road
13	James Whittle	40 Thwaites Street
14	Patterson Oates & Sons	14 Blackburn Road
15	William Clegg	75 Mount Street
16	William Davenport	113 Darley Street
17	John Eccleshaw	131 Darley Street
18	Edward Castle	8 Victor Street
19	Miss Alice Brown	95 Tonge Moor Road
20	Samuel Eccles	78 Markland Hill Lane
		(off the map)
21	Henry Holden	81 Tonge Moor Road
22	James Lomax	111 Higher Bridge Street
23	Patterson Oates & Sons	Back Turton Street

24	Samuel Crowther	40 Turton Street
25	John Martindale	175 Chorley Old Road
26	George Langdon	30 School Hill
27	Mrs Elizabeth Smith	182 Folds Road
28	Miss Emma Walmsley	169 Chorley Old Road
29	John Waterhouse	83 Vernon Street
30	Fred Openshaw	55 Higher Bridge Street
31	Walter Russell	62 Folds Road
32	Christopher Isherwood	101 Chorley Old Road

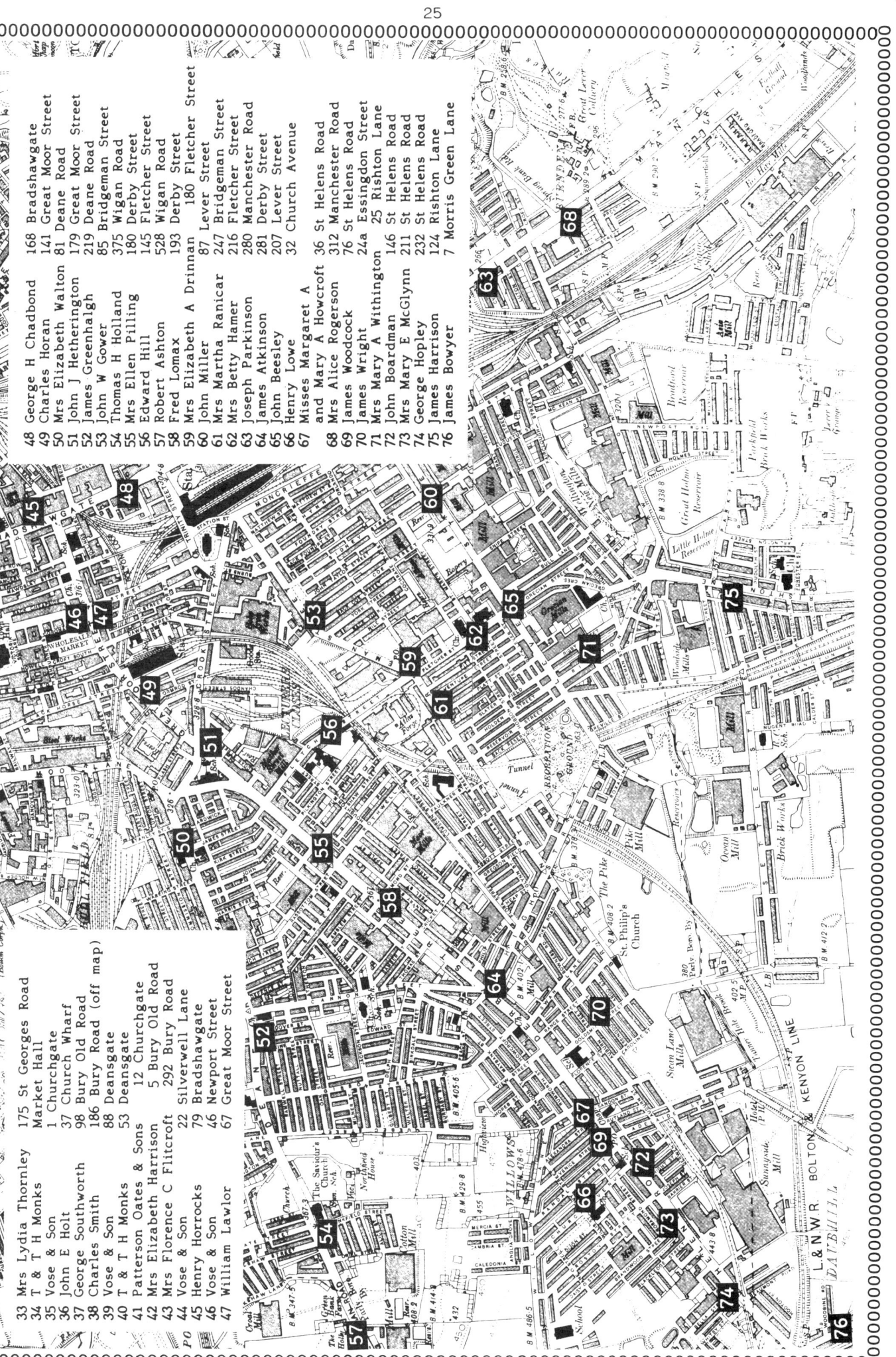

48 George H Chadbond 168 Bradshawgate
49 Charles Horan 141 Great Moor Street
50 Mrs Elizabeth Walton 81 Deane Road
51 John J Hetherington 179 Great Moor Street
52 James Greenhalgh 219 Deane Road
53 John W Gower 85 Bridgeman Street
54 Thomas H Holland 375 Wigan Road
55 Mrs Ellen Pilling 180 Derby Street
56 Edward Hill 145 Fletcher Street
57 Robert Ashton 528 Wigan Road
58 Fred Lomax 193 Derby Street
59 Mrs Elizabeth A Drinnan 180 Fletcher Street
60 John Miller 87 Lever Street
61 Mrs Martha Ranicar 247 Bridgeman Street
62 Mrs Betty Hamer 216 Fletcher Street
63 Joseph Parkinson 280 Manchester Road
64 James Atkinson 281 Derby Street
65 John Beesley 207 Lever Street
66 Henry Lowe 32 Church Avenue
67 Misses Margaret A
   and Mary A Howcroft 36 St Helens Road
68 Mrs Alice Rogerson 312 Manchester Road
69 James Woodcock 76 St Helens Road
70 James Wright 24a Essingdon Street
71 Mrs Mary A Withington 25 Rishton Lane
72 John Boardman 146 St Helens Road
73 Mrs Mary E McGlynn 211 St Helens Road
74 George Hopley 232 St Helens Road
75 James Harrison 124 Rishton Lane
76 James Bowyer 7 Morris Green Lane

33 Mrs Lydia Thornley 175 St Georges Road
34 T & T H Monks Market Hall
35 Vose & Son 1 Churchgate
36 John E Holt 37 Church Wharf
37 George Southworth 98 Bury Old Road
38 Charles Smith 186 Bury Road (off map)
39 Vose & Son 88 Deansgate
40 T & T H Monks 53 Deansgate
41 Patterson Oates & Sons 12 Churchgate
42 Mrs Elizabeth Harrison 5 Bury Old Road
43 Mrs Florence C Flitcroft 292 Bury Old Road
44 Vose & Son 22 Silverwell Lane
45 Henry Horrocks 79 Bradshawgate
46 Vose & Son 46 Newport Street
47 William Lawlor 67 Great Moor Street

MASON R Ltd, Exmouth St; branches: 95 West-
gate; 26 St James' St; 53 Yorkshire St;
97 Manchester Rd; 88 Curzon St; 3 & 42a
Briercliffe Rd; 68 Trafalgar St; 225 Acc-
rington Rd; 155 Oxford Rd; 58 Abel St; 35
Brougham St; 316 Colne Rd; 95 Coal Clough
La; 3 Rose Grove La; 40 Lyndhurst Rd; &
313 Padiham Rd, Burnley; 23a & 87 Leeds
Rd; 74 Manchester Rd; 1 Market Hall
buildings, Every Street & 15 Railway St,
Nelson; 135 Burnley Rd, Padiham, Burnley
& 31 Church Street, Blackburn
MASSEY E, 81 Deane Road, Bolton
MATTHEW O, 304 Eccles New Road, Salford
MAYHALL & TOMKINSON, River Bank Works,
Arkley, Warrington (& wholesale)
MELLOR S A, 54 Radcliffe Street, Oldham
MERCER J, 3 New Hall Lane, Preston
MILLER G H, 44 King Street, Salford
MILLER Mrs M, 87 Lever Street, Bolton
MILLER William, 34 Ronald Street, Oldham
MILLIGAN Mrs J, 96 Halliwell La, Cheetham
MILLS A, 15 Topley St, Rochdale Road, M/c
MILLS Mrs A, 195 Ellor Street, Pendleton
MILLS J R, 3 Rochdale Road, Shaw, Oldham
MILLS R, 13 Vavasour Street, Rochdale
MITCHELL James, 221 Stockport Rd, Longsight
MITCHELL J Ltd, 79 Dearden Gate, Haslingden
MITCHELL G, 24 Salford, Clitheroe
MITCHELL J E, Cotton Tree Lane, Colne
MITTY J Ltd, office & works, 34-46 Naylor
St; stables & garage 24&26 Naylor St,
Vauxhall Rd; 186 Gt Homer St; 5 Smith St;
40 Robson St; 24 Paddington; 258 Kensing-
ton; 144 Wavertree Rd; 22 West Derby Rd;
270 West Derby Rd, Tuebrook; 183 Stanley
Rd; 105 Picton Rd, Wavertree; 145 Breck
Rd, Anfield; 111 Lodge La, Liverpool: 56
& 149 Grange Rd & 143 Conway St, Birken-
head, & 32 Brighton St, Seacombe
MOLEY J, 156 & 245 Oldham Road, Manchester
MONK G Ltd, Monk Street, Blackburn
MONK G, 84 Copy Nook & 59 Harwood Street,
Blackburn
MONK Gideon, 8 Water St, Great Harwood
MONK T H, 182 Folds Road, Bolton
MONKS E, 177 Radnor Street, Hulme, M/cr
MONKS Kay, 33 Bridge Street, Ramsbottom
MOORE J T, 3 Ainsworth Street, Blackburn
MORTON Mrs E, 10 Clowes St, W Gorton, M/c
MORTON G, 264a Bolton Rd North, Ramsbottom
MOSS G, 8 Blackburn Road, Darwen
MOSS Tom, 162 Brinksway, Stockport
MULLIGAN T, 481 Rochdale Road, Manchester

1900 advertisement

NADEN C, 99 Stockport Rd, Ashton-under-Lyne
NEEDHAM Fred, 552 Ashton Old Road, Openshaw
NEILL Mrs E, 22 Ashton Rd, Droylsden, M/c
NELSON T, 17 Nugent Rd, Great Lever, Bolton
NEWMAN Fred, 66 Lees Road, Oldham
NICHOLLS J, 16 Chester Sq, Ashton-u-Lyne
NICHOLSON T H, 57 Albert Road, Farnworth
NIELD J, 72 Warwick St, Werneth, Oldham
NUTTALL A, 98 Union Street, Oldham
NUTTALL H 42 Victoria St, Littleborough
NUTTALL L, 18 Mumps & 94 Huddersfield Road,
Oldham
NUTTALL Miss M, 177 Burnley Rd, Rawtenstall

O'BRIEN J, 108b Whitworth Road, Rochdale
OGDEN Mrs E A, 129 Church Street, Pendleton
OGDEN Harry, 32 Preston Street, Hulme, M/cr
OGDEN R, 2 Chapel St, Cheetham Hill, M/c
O'HARA E, 91 Cross St, Ashton-on-Mersey
OLDHAM Ellis, 373 Buxton Road, Stockport
OLDHAM T, 77a Stockport Rd, Ashton-u-Lyne
ORMROD Richard, 81 Beswick St, Ancoats, M/c

OSWALD Mrs A, 214 Chester Road, Hulme, M/cr
OWEN R, 108 Mornington Road, Bolton
OWEN W E, 43 Upper Jackson St, Hulme, M/cr

PALMER J H, 99 Hyde Rd, Woodley, Stockport
PARK Mrs E, 35 Whelley, Wigan
PARKER John, 150 Ellor Street, Pendleton
PARKER WALKER Ltd, 53 Princess St, Bury, &
28 Crostons Rd, Elton, Bury
PARKHOUSE C, 655 Stockport Rd, Longsight
PARKIN A W, 6 Coronation Walk, Southport
PARKINSON A, 13 Corporation St, St Helens
PARTINGTON F C, 4 Upper Moss La, Hulme, M/c
PATTERSON J, Ramsden Rd, Wardle, Rochdale
PEARCE William, 40 Dove Lane, Darwen
PEARSON John, 38 Regent Road, Salford
PEARSON W&J, Bamber Bridge, Preston
PEARSON J, 729 Hollins Road, Hollinwood
PEARSON E, 334 Liverpool Rd, Patricroft
PELL PEERS, 142 Heaton La, Heaton Norris
PENDLEBURY E, 1155 Chester Road, Stretford
PENDLEBURY J R, Simpson St, Bradford, M/c;
347 Ashton New Rd, Bradford; 328 Ashton
Old Rd, Openshaw; 21 & 107 Stretford Rd,
Hulme; 319 Hyde Rd, Ardwick; 89 Queens Rd,
Harpurhey; 107 Oldham St & 254 Queens Rd,
Miles Platting
PETIFORD R, 32 Waterside Road, Colne
PHILLIPS J T, 44 King St West, Stockport
PICKUP G, 90a Bank Street, Rawtenstall
PICKUP Miss M E, 29 Winston Rd, Blackburn
PILLING C, 102 Manchester St & 139 York St,
Heywood
PILLING Mrs H, 75 Sandy Lane, Heaton Norris
PILLING R, 12&72 Church St; 112 Bury St; 11
Bridge St; 24 Market St & 3 Rochdale Rd E,
Heywood
PILLING Mrs S, 19 Withington St, Heywood
PILLING T, 147 Crescent Rd, Gt Lever, Bolton
PLATT A E, 320 Ashton Road, Oldham
PLATT E, 69 Eastbank Street, Southport
PLATT Fred, High Crompton, Shaw, Oldham
PLATT T, 11 Wakefield Road, Stalybridge
PLATT Wm, 224 Oldham Road, Failsworth, M/c
POLLITT J, 129 Ridgway Street, Ancoats, M/c
POLLITT Mrs P, 14 Station Road, Swinton
POOLE C E, 5 North George Street, Salford
POOLE Mrs C, 66 Gorton La, West Gorton, M/c
POWELL M J, 289 Ashton Old Rd, Ardwick, M/c
POWNALL Mrs D, 63 London Rd, Hazel Grove
POWNALL E, 194 Crab La, Hr Blackley, M/cr
PRATT A, 5 Wellington St, Stockport
PRICE H, 62 Ashton New Rd, Beswick, M/cr
PRIOR H, 74 Ormskirk Rd, Newtown, Wigan
PROCTOR E, 62 Folds Road, Bolton
PULPHER E E, 99 Castle St, Edgeley, Stk'pt
PYRAH F, 542 Oldham Rd, Manchester, & 670
Oldham Road, Failsworth

QUINN J W, 133b Blackburn Road, Accrington

RADCLIFFE E, 20 Snig Brook, Blackburn
RADCLIFFE W H, 119 High St, Lees, Oldham
RADFORD W, 372 Grimshaw La, Middleton Jct
RATCLIFF R, 41 Uppr Medlock St, Hulme, M/cr
RATCLIFFE G, Argyle St, Accrington
REEVES J, 29 Kenyon La, Moston, Manchester
RENSHAW F, 2 Oldham Rd, Failsworth, M/c
REVENS H, 19 Manchester Road, Haslingden
RHODES A, 13 Milkstone Road, Rochdale
RHODES H, 107 Oldham Rd; Stuart St; 84
Spotland Rd; 11 Milkstone Rd & 4 Lord St,
Rochdale
RIDEHALGH B, 36 High St, Rishton, B'burn
RIDGWAY A, 48 Victoria St, Ashton-u-Lyne

John Sherlock's tripe shop on Tatton Street, Salford, in the 1920s

RIDGWAY B, 73 Old Rd, Heaton Norris, Stkp't
RIDING Charles, 203 Liverpool St, Salford
RIDYARD R, 1 & 133 Cross St, Gorton; 166
    Wilmslow Rd, Fallowfield; 1 Church Lane,
    Gorton, & 89 Embden St, Hulme, M/cr
RIDYARD R, 64 Gorton Rd, Reddish, Stockport
RIGBY R, 422 Bolton Road, Blackburn
RILEY J W, 17 Thorp Rd, Newton Heath, M/cr
RILEY Mrs M, 84 Westfield St, St Helens
RILEY Walter, 168 Shaw Road, Oldham
RILEY Wm, 606 Burnley Road, Crawshawbooth
RITCHIE J, 168 Bradshawgate, Bolton
ROBERTS A, 296 Oldham Road, Manchester
ROBERTS J, 192 Redlam, Blackburn
ROBERTS M A, 70 Conran St, Harpurhey, M/cr
ROBERTS T, 52 Bury Old Rd, Heaton Park, M/c
ROBINSON E, 46 Adelphi St; 176 Marsh La &
    180 Ribbleton Lane, Preston
ROBINSON James, 64 Bridge Street, Bury
RODGERS C M, 132 Ashton Road, Oldham
ROSCOW A, 83 Tyldesley Rd, Atherton
ROSTRON T, 68 Market Street, Farnworth
ROWARTH E, 84 Wilmslow Rd, Rusholme, M/c
ROWBOTHAM J, 34 Gt Portwood St, Stockport
ROWLSTONE A, 412 Stretford Rd, Hulme, M/cr
ROYDS A, 226 Bamford Road, Heywood
ROYLE T, 492 Liverpool Road, Patricroft
RUSCOE M, 300 Bolton Rd, Irlams o'th'Height
RUSCOE R, 97 Lower Broughton Rd, Salford
RUSSELL Mrs C, 77 Collyhurst St, Manchester

SAGAR T, 151 Padiham Road, Burnley
SCHOFIELD G E, 32 Wilmslow Rd, Rusholme,M/c
SCHOFIELD J A, 658 Oldham Rd, Newton Heath
SCHOLES Ellis, 140 Mount Street, Bolton
SCHOLES F, 159 Guide Lane, Audenshaw, M/cr
SCRAGG Mrs M, 252 Rathbone Rd, Wavertree
SEANOR G, 8 Oldham Rd, Miles Platting, M/cr
SEED Mrs E, 224 Waterloo Rd, Crumpsall, M/c
SHACKLETON M, 127 Dalton Rd, Barrow-in-F'ss
SHARPLES John, 522 Bolton Road, Darwen
SHARPLES J, 60 New Chapel St, Blackburn
SHARPLES J, 31 Park Road, Blackburn
SHAW A, 270 Whalley Old Road, Blackburn
SHAW H, 33 Great Portwood St, Stockport
SHAW Richard, 53 Park Road, Preston
SHEARD A A, 43 Shakespeare Street, Padiham
SHEARS J, 96 Union Rd, Oswaldtwistle
SHEPHARD A B, 17 Whit Lane, Pendleton
SHEPHARD W, 119 Bradford Rd, Ancoats, M/cr
SHERLOCK J, 115 Tatton Street, Salford
SHERRATT Mrs M, 34 Hankinson St, Pendleton
SHUTT M & Mrs E, 70 Abbey St, Accrington
SHUTTLEWORTH W, 59 Plungington Rd, Preston
SIDEBOTTOM J, 63 Acres La; 17 Stamford St &
    19 Mottram Road, Stalybridge
SIDEBOTTOM T, 12 Manchester Rd, Mossley,M/c
SIMISTER A, 62 Bolton Road, Walkden
SIMPSON E, 238 Huddersfield Rd, Oldham
SIMMONS F J, 189 Chapel Street, Salford
SIMMONS J F, 27 Camp St, Lower Broughton
SIMMONS J F, 80 Stockport Rd, Longsight,M/c
SINGLETON George, 81 Nuttall St, Accrington
SKEET J, 513 Bolton Rd, Pendlebury
SLINGER Mrs M, 78 New Hall Lane, Preston
SLOAN Hugh, 91 Stuart St, Bradford, M/cr
SMALLEY S, 6 Ashton New Rd, Beswick, M/c
SMETHURST A, 111 Butler St, Oldham Rd, M/c
SMITH C, 206 Bury Road, Bolton
SMITH C, 312 Manchester Road, Bolton
SMITH F, 127 Partington Lane, Swinton
SMITH G, 17 Cooper Street, Withington
SMITH Jane, 111 Cross St, Ashton-on-Mersey
SMITH J, 35 Earle Street, Earlestown
SMITH J, 723 Ormskirk Rd, Pemberton, Wigan
SMITH J, 10 Bradford Street, Ancoats, M/c
SMITH J W, 335 Moston Lane, Moston, M/cr
SMITH T, 175 Ridgway Street, Ancoats, M/cr
SMITH W, 78 Barnes St, Clayton-le-Moors
SMITHIES W&A, Argyle Street, Accrington
SNELLING H, 7 Arthur St, East Crompton,Shaw
SNOWDEN James, 88 Scotland Road, Nelson
SOUTHWORTH R, Croft St; 3 Cross St & 111
    Abbey Street, Accrington
SOWERBUTTS H, 463 Manchester Road, Baxenden
SPEAK H, 4 Harbour Lane, Milnrow, Rochdale
SPEAK W, 145 Love La, Heaton Norris, Stkp't
STAVELEY I, 52 Brook Street, C-on-M, M/cr
STEEL E G, 292 Colne Road, Burnley
STEVENS E, 20 New Park Road, Salford
STOBART E L, 151 Eccles New Road, Salford

STOREY E, Tithebarn St, Poulton-le-Fylde
STOTT H, 113 Belgrave Rd, New Moston, M/cr
STOTT R, 103 Central Drive, Blackpool
STREET F, 21 Stockport Rd, Levenshulme, M/c
STUBBS A, 18 Gilda Brook Road, Eccles
STURGESS W H, 1 Bold Street, Accrington
SULLIVAN J, 161 Queen Street, Preston
SULLIVAN M A, 18 Lancaster Road, Preston
SUTCLIFFE F J, Gauxholme & 19 Rochdale Rd,
    Todmorden
SUTCLIFFE James, 149 Scholes, Wigan
SUTTON A, 1 Exchange Street, Blackley
SUTTON Mrs H, 24 London Road, Preston
SWARBRICK L, 31&33 St Petersgate, Stockport
SWARBRICK William, 33 Leeds Road, Nelson
SWINDELLS Wm, 28 Queen Street, Morecambe

TALBOT G, 4 Sudell Cross, Blackburn
TAYLOR A, 102 Liverpool Street, Salford
TAYLOR A, 132 Oxford St, Werneth, Oldham
TAYLOR C, 83 Adelphi Street, Preston
TAYLOR E, 402 Ashton Old Rd, Openshaw, M/cr
TAYLOR E, 4 Haslingden Road, Rawtenstall
TAYLOR E, 179 Katherine St, Ashton-u-Lyne
TAYLOR G, 133 Lower Broughton Rd, Salford
TAYLOR W H, 28 Westfield St, St Helens
TAYLOR W H, 86 St John's Market, Liverpool
TERRY H, 84 Burnley Road, Colne
THOMPSON M A, 3 Oldham Rd, Ashton-u-Lyne
THORP E, 116 Reddish Lane, Gorton, M/cr
TICKLE J, 95 Duke Street, St Helens
TICKLE M E, 7 Covered Market, St Helens
TILSTON Wm, 97 Wood Street, Middleton
TIMMINS P, 65 Glebe St, East Crompton, Shaw
TONGE Ralph, 24 Deane Road, Bolton
TOOTELL J & Sons, 37 Market Street, Chorley
TOOTELL W & Sons, 20 Bolton Street, Chorley
TOWLER Stanley, 73 Bridge Street, Heywood
TOWNLEY Henry, 259 Union Rd, Oswaldtwistle
TURNER James, 19 Cross Lane, Gorton, M/cr
TURNER R, 120 Hillgate St, Hurst Pk, A-u-L
TURNER W A, 11 Oxford Road, Burnley
TYSON A, 182 Moss La E, Moss Side, M/cr

UDALL A E, 5 Albert Place, Manchester
UNITED CATTLE PRODUCTS Ltd, 8 Colne Road,
    Brierfield, Burnley; 6 Church St, Colne &
    4a Park Street, Lytham
UNSWORTH A, 58 Manch'r Rd W, Little Hulton
UNSWORTH G P, 498 Blackburn Road, Bolton

VOSE & SON, 22 Silverwell La; 1 Churchgate;
    46 Newport St; 281 Derby St; 464 Black-
    burn Rd; 79 Bradshawgate; 53 & 88 Deans-
    gate; 43 Hr Bridge St & 81 Tonge Moor Rd,
    Bolton; 67 Hr Market St, Kearsley; 29
    Market St, Leigh; 133 Elliott St, Tyldes-
    ley & 164 Manchester Road, Higher Ince
VOSE John R, 113 Blackburn St, Radcliffe
VALENTINE W, 103 Longden Rd, Longsight, M/c

WADDICOR J, 86 Duckworth Street, Darwen
WADSWORTH W, 1178 Burnley Rd, Love Clough
WAITE H, 77 Travis St, London Rd,Manchester
WAKEFIELD H, 63 Stockport Rd, Longsight,M/c
WALKDEN Mrs A, 173 Whit Lane, Pendleton
WALKER A, 180 Gt Jackson St, Hulme, M/cr
WALKER E, 22 Ainsworth Rd, Radcliffe
WALKER E, 191 Rochdale Road, Bury
WALKER L, 25 Oak Street, Moston, Manchester
WALKER R, Argyle Street, Accrington
WALLACE J R, 9 Edward Street, Stockport
WALLEY W, 27 Waterloo St, Lwr Crumpsall,M/c
WALMSLEY E, 169 Chorley Old Rd, Bolton
WALMSLEY S, 67 Shaw Heath, Stockport
WALMSLEY W, 83 Derby Street, Bolton
WALSH I, 86 Lancashire Hill, Stockport
WALSH N, 791 Rochdale Road, Manchester
WALSH W R, Argyle St & 25 Devonshire St,
    Accrington
WALTON J, 53 Stockport Rd, Romiley, Stkp't
WARD J, 191 Queens Rd, Crumpsall, M/cr
WARD M A, 453 Chorley Old Road, Bolton
WARING A, 229 North Road, Preston
WARING T, 5 Moston La, Barnes Green, M/cr
WARREN A, 199 Ordsall Lane, Salford
WATKISON J S, 392 Eccles New Road, Salford
WATTS E, 3 Oldfield Road, Salford
WEIKERT R, 204 Whit Lane, Pendleton
WETHERBY M, 138 Chapel Lane, Wigan
WHIP J, 98 Eastbank Street, Southport
WHIPP E, 1 Firwood St, Middleton Junction

WHITAKER M A, 12 Gorton Rd, Reddish, Stkp't
WHITEHEAD R, 335 Ripponden Rd, Oldham
WHITEHEAD S, 118 Dale St, Milnrow, Rochdale
WHITEHEAD W, 150 M/cr Rd E, Little Hulton
WHITEMAN J, 207 Lever Street, Bolton
WHITHAM J, 54 Silk Street, Salford
WHITTAKER E, 21 Exchange Street, Colne
WHITTAKER F, 155a Accrington Rd, Burnley
WHITTAKER J, 62 Bridge Street, Ramsbottom
WHITTAKER J, 31 Gannow La, Burnley
WHITTAKER J, 6 Moss Lane, Pendlebury
WHITTAM M, 45 Glynne Street, Farnworth
WHITTLE T, 5 Church St, Gt Harwood, Bolton
WILBRAHAM A, 201 Liverpool Road, Patricroft
WILCOX H, 116 Church Street, Preston
WILD A & A, 5 Henshaw Street, Oldham
WILD S E, 129 Manchester Street, Oldham
WILDE A, 178a Middleton Road, Oldham
WILKINSON J E, 30 Walmersley Road, Bury
WILKINSON J W, 244 M/cr Rd E, Little Hulton
WILLIAMS A, 31 Pendle Street, Nelson
WILLIAMS A, 453 Stockport Rd, Longsight,M/c
WILLIAMS K, 56 Foxhall Road, Blackpool
WILLIAMSON F W, 130 Hr Hillgate, Stockport
WILLIAMSON H, 122 Oldham Rd, Waterloo,A-u-L
WILLIAMSON J B, 5 Market Place, Clitheroe
WILLS L, 290 City Road, Hulme, Manchester
WILSON J E, 89 Higher Bridge St, Bolton
WILSON M, 373 Rochdale Road, Manchester
WINDER H, 29 Hesketh St, Heaton Norris
WINTERBOTTOM F, 134 Glodwick Rd & 32 Hudd-
    ersfield Rd, Oldham
WINTERBOTTOM L, 115 Trafford Road, Salford
WITHINGTON M A, 23 Rishton Lane, Bolton
WOOD A, 59 Castle St, Edgeley, Stockport
WOOD E, 84 Gt Portwood St, Stockport
WOOD W, 132 Oldham Rd, Rochdale
WOODBURN R, 101 London Road, Preston
WOOLLEY D, 31 Croft St & 582 Ashton New Rd,
    Clayton, Manchester
WORRALL H, 179 Langworthy Road, Salford
WORSICK J, 62 Market St, Colne
WORSTENCROFT H, 149 Drury La, Hollinwood
WORSWICK A, 7 Morris Green Lane, Bolton
WORSWICK W H, 10 St Davids Rd S, St Annes
WORTHINGTON J, 43 Stamford St, Mossley, M/c
WRIGHT T&H, 27&29 Marybone; Back Pickop St
    & 2 Prescot Street, Liverpool
WRIGHT W, 3 Coalshaw Green Rd, Hollinwood
WROE G, 129 St Hubert's Rd, Great Harwood
WYCHE R C, 74 Radnor St, Hulme, Manchester

YARWOOD M, 78 High St, Rishton, Blackburn
YATES B, 148 Waterloo Street, Oldham
YATES J, 89 Regent Road, Salford
YOUNG T C, 3 Rusholme Rd, C-on-M,Manchester
YOUNG W, 3 Eagle St, Accrington

Part 4
Bolton - 'Trotter Town'

The Bolton Evening News of 2nd April 1951 carried a short article on the origin of the nickname of Bolton Wanderers:
"Trotter has nothing to do with an animal - it is the old-time description of the man from 'Trottertown', and 'Bolton Trotters' were so named, it is said, after a hoax or 'trot' played on a visitor.

An oil painting used to hang in the Bar Parlour of the Swan Hotel showing a man with a wooden leg, which he held in a bucket of hot water. The visitor had been drawn into a wager as to who could hold a leg in the water the longest. Such practical jokes were the essence of Bolton trotting. Bolton Wanderers became, in local parlance, the 'Trotters'. Some, however, prefer to stick to the perhaps more logical explanation that it is derived from the Boltonians' liking for trotters and cowheels, and - 'What more suitable symbol than a sheep's foot from the tripe shop?' So today in Bolton, edible trotters are sheep's feet. Some (mostly from the South) think a trotter is a pig's foot; little use to point out that a pig's progress little resembles the quick movement of a sheep. But in this town of trotting, trotters are trotters and pigs' feet are pigs' feet. This is confirmed by 'Tum o' Dick o' Bob's' in his 'Lankisher Dickshionary', by the explanation that 'A trotter is a sheep's foot, boiled'."

In 1902 Charles Roeder published "Notes on Food and Drink in Lancashire and the Northern Counties" in the Lancashire and Cheshire Antiquarian Society's journal. In the article he quoted Ben Brierley:"*'Pig-killin' in Lancashire was a great family affair ... We have the nottlins familiar in Bolton, which was 'th' bally o'th'pig beight into tripe'.*" Familiar it may have been, but I have never heard the term "nottlins" used in Bolton!

Judging from the number of advertisers in local directories from the nineteenth century onwards, there have certainly been enough purveyors of tripe products in Bolton to satisfy the town's working population.

One of the earliest references to tripe dealing in the town is an advertisement which appeared in the Bolton Express of 27th September 1823:

"Peter Heron - Tripe Dealer, Top of Taylor Brow, Deansgate, Begs to express his sincere acknowledgements for the very liberal Support he has received from his Friends and the Public in general since his commencing the above Business, and assures his customers that no attention shall be wanting on his part to maintain the high name his TRIPE has acquired for its prime and superior qualities.

Peter Heron takes this opportunity to inform his Friends, that he can supply them with TRIPE, HEELS, &c as usual, at his Shop every Friday, and Sunday Evenings at 7 o'clock.

NB. Calves' Heads prepared for Mock Turtle."

The Bolton Directory for 1836 records "Robert Haslam, Leather and Tripe Dealer." (This directory also lists a certain Giles Vose, Blacksmith – perhaps a relative of the "Tripe Voses"?) The directories for 1841, 1843 and 1849 give more names, three or four at most, and there is some evidence to suggest that tripe dressers may have preferred to be designated

1885 advertisement

1892 advertisement

under other trades, such as "butcher", "provision dealer" or even "waste dealer". For example, the 1843 directory cites "Robert & Peter Haslam, Leather and Neats-foot oil dealers", with no mention of tripe at all; in 1849 they are listed under "Tripe Dressers". Again, in the 1843 directory there is a Thomas Lever, butcher, of Moor Lane; in 1853 he is classed as a tripe dresser. Six other tripe dressers are recorded in Bolton in 1853: Edmund Barlow of Shipgates, William Fletcher of Folds Road, William Haslam of Deansgate, Robert Monks of Hulme Street, Ellis Ratcliffe of Bradshawgate and Henry Waters of Lum Street.

From the 1870s there was a marked increase in the number of tripe dressers and dealers; by the turn of the century there were more than 50, some with several shops or market stalls. By the year 1911 there were over 70 names listed in the local trade directory.

Inevitably, there were some failures, and one such was reported in the Bolton Journal of 21st March 1902. Under the heading "A Tripe Dealer's Failure", it was related thus:

"A meeting of the creditors of Joseph Nuttall, 67, Great Moor Street, tripe dealer, was held on Wednesday at the office of the Official Receiver, Mr T H Winder, Exchange Street.

The debtor's statement of affairs showed liabilities amounting to £278 and assets £170, leaving a deficiency of £107. The causes of failure were alleged by the debtor to be trade losses, loss by death of a horse and loss by accident. In his observation of the case the Official Receiver said the bankrupt was a tripe dresser by trade, and for the last five years he had also been a retail tripe dealer. In April 1900 he became tenant of a tripe dressing works in Back Spring Gardens, Bolton. The working utensils there belonged to the landlord. The business was conducted at a loss, and the bankrupt became unable to pay his accounts.."

Joseph Nuttall had been in the tripe business since at least 1871, when he worked for his father, Henry, at 121 Deansgate. He was then aged 15, and was already designated a tripe dresser. Ten years earlier the shop had been run by Peter Higson, another tripe dresser. Higson was in business at 86 Spring Gardens in 1871 and

around 1894/5 he moved to St Helens Road, Over Hulton, probably to retire.

Joseph's progress was evidently not as fortuitous. After the death of his father, his mother Elizabeth took over the business in the early 1880s. In 1896 Joseph had a shop at 153 Deansgate and by 1902 he was residing at 220 Derby Street and renting the ill-fated tripe works in Back Spring Gardens. His sister Mary was running the Deansgate shop.

Perhaps Joseph rented the tripe works from his more successful predecessor, Peter Higson, and it was Higson who instituted the bankruptcy proceedings.

So the tripe business, like any other, had its pitfalls and not everyone made a fortune from the trade. Certainly, there were easier ways of making a living!

Under the Public Health Act of 1875, anyone wishing to pursue the "offensive trade" of tripe boiling in Bolton had to have the permission of Bolton Corporation. By 1895 the Corporation Sanitary Committee were of the opinion that there were enough tripe boilers in the town, which was unfortunate for Great and Little Bolton Co-operative Society

1881 advertisement

1885 advertisement

Ltd. In the February of that year the Inspector of Nuisance, Mr Spencer, visited the Co-op slaughterhouses in All Saints Street and found that tripe was being boiled. A charge was brought against the Society at a meeting of Bolton Justices in the April.

The Society evidently considered that it was worth defending the charge, and a Mr Fielding appeared before the magistrates on its behalf. His argument was that there was, in fact, no case to answer *"...inasmuch as they did not carry on the trade of tripe boiling. They simply bought cows alive, slaughtered them and, to prevent waste, converted the offal into tripe. They were merely butchers, and the boiling of bellies was incidental to the business of a butcher. True, the Co-operative Society had applied for a licence for...tripe boiling; but ...by having such a licence they could buy bellies from whom they wished and convert them into tripe. The Corporation in their wisdom - and he never saw a more intelligent lot of men in his life - said; 'We will not allow them to carry on tripe boiling', and therefore the Co-operative Society were prevented from treating with other butchers for the purchase of their bellies.*

The definition of trade was buying and selling; and only utilising the bellies of their own cows...did not constitute buying. They simply boiled what was their own, and they did not buy the bellies for the purpose of making tripe. If a conviction took place...they would have to throw the offal away, and this would be a monstrous and iniquitous waste."

The magistrates were not convinced by Mr Fielding's argument and they decided in favour of the Corporation, fining the Co-op ten shillings and costs.

Having failed to set up their own tripe manufactory, the Co-op lost no time in finding an existing business to take over. By June 1896 they were renting, at 10/- per week, a tripe boiling works at 4 Back Derby Street; the working plant was purchased from the previous tenant, George Cain. From July 6th tripe and cowheels were being boiled and offered for sale in the Society's shops - "unapproachable for quality and freshness".

In 1901 the owner of the tripe works, Robert Hilton, sold out and it became the property of the Co-op. There was a complete plant for tripe boiling and also tallow refining (nothing was wasted!), consisting of vertical boiler, tripe pans and tallow vats.

Just when this tripe works closed is uncertain, but Bolton Co-op hasn't done any tripe boiling since before the War, although several Co-operative Societies in the North were members of the National Association of Tripedressers until the late 1950s.

Some Bolton Tripe Families

Voses

The name Vose was once a household word for miles around. From modest beginnings the family's tripe business expanded to such an extent that by the time it was taken over by the UCP there was a tripe works and more than a dozen retail outlets throughout the district.

The Vose (or Vause) family came originally from the Horwich and Chorley areas, where they had been involved in the cotton trade. James and Helen Vause had several offspring, of whom Thomas (born 1813), Elizabeth and Robert (born at Blackrod in 1814 and 1820) and John (born at Chorley, 1828) are relevant to this story.

Some time in the 1830s the family moved to Bolton, where James started up as a coal merchant; his son Robert was a farrier and John was a dyer by trade.

Around this time there lived in Rawson's Court a waste dealer named Jonathan Ratcliffe. His son Ellis married Elizabeth Vose in August 1837. Ellis, like his father, dealt in "waste", and by 1853, when he was living in Bradshawgate, his trade was classed as tripedressing. Two years later Robert Vose, blacksmith, married Elizabeth Seddon.

In 1861 the Ratcliffes resided at 1 Churchgate, with business premises on Bradshawgate. Four years later Robert Vose was recorded at both these addresses and the 1871 Census confirms that the entire Vose family and their servants were living at the Churchgate address. What had happened to Ellis Ratcliffe is unclear, but one may assume that Robert Vose had taken over the tripe business from his brother-in-law.

Robert and Elizabeth Vose were blessed with four children: Alice (1856), Robert junior (1857), Ellen (1862) and Elizabeth Ann (1866). Elizabeth Vose died not long after the birth of Elizabeth Ann, and after a suitable period had elapsed, Robert married Jane Dickenson, who had previously worked for Ellis Ratcliffe. She had a son, Thomas, who in 1881 was 18-years-old and working as a pawnbroker's assistant.

1894 advertisement

In 1881 Robert junior was aged 23, unmarried and employed by his father as a tripedresser at their works on Silverwell Lane, back of Bradshawgate. He married (yet another Elizabeth!) and took a house on Wood Street.

Robert Vose died at the then ripe old age of 74, followed only a year later by his son. Robert Vose senior left his shop and dwelling house on the corner of Churchgate and Bank Street to be disposed of by his trustees, with the provision that his daughter Elizabeth be allowed to live there for two years after his death and afterwards *"be at liberty to purchase the premises ... for £1,000, and the furniture and effects ... for such a sum as shall have been valued at..."*

The tripedressing business itself, Robert Vose & Son, survived the deaths of its founder and his son and expanded during the first two decades of this century. Several retail shops were acquired in Bolton (in Newport Street, Deansgate, Blackburn Road, Derby Street, Halliwell Road, Chorley Old Road, St George's Road, Lever Street and Higher Bridge Street) and elsewhere.

Robert Vose & Son Ltd became part of the UCP in 1920, but the family name lived on for many years afterwards. A condition of the merger was that "Voses" should continue to appear on shop fronts, along

with the familiar UCP trade mark.

In 1922 Elizabeth Ann Fryer (nee Vose) was still living at the Churchgate shop.

What of Thomas Vose, James Vose's eldest son? He made his way to Radcliffe, at first pursuing the bleaching trade. But soon he too started in business as a tripedresser, in Blackburn Street. Why he went to Radcliffe rather than Bolton is something of a mystery, but whatever the reason, it seems that he kept up his family ties, hence the venture into what must have become a highly profitable line of work.

Charlie Smith's

Another well-known Bolton firm of tripedressers and tripesellers was that of Smiths of Bury Road. The firm was begun by Charles Smith in the 1870s, and "Charlie Smith's", as it was known locally, flourished until just after the Second World War.

Charles had a large family, but only two sons – the eldest child, Charles, and the youngest, John – carried on the business. The Smiths had their own lorries, which collected supplies of bellies from Trinity Street Station and also delivered the dressed tripe to outlying areas as far away as Eccles and Worsley. As a rule the tripes came from Scotland, and in particular those from Murray's of Aberdeen were universally acknowledged to be of excellent quality.

At Smith's tripe works the bellies were first put into cast iron tanks and steam jets played on to the tripes to clean them. Then they were placed on "scraping tables" where the skins were scraped off by hand. Then they were put into a second boiling tank, to which vitriol and peroxide were added to whiten them. From there the tripes were transferred to tanks of iced water to cool off.

Cowheels and trotters were treated in roughly the same way; the hooves were taken off and sent for fertilizer; bones went for bonemeal. The skins were put into a press and neatsfoot oil was extracted. The fat which was taken off the tops of the tanks was sold as dripping.

In the "settlement pits", where the slops and excess water ran, the fatty scourings from the

Voses shop on the corner of Churchgate in the early 1900s

boilings were sold as tallow for candle-making. A small stock of hooves was also kept, as these were ideal for breeding maggots. The maggots were regularly sold to local fishermen.

Elder, which resembles a yellowish-coloured football, was also boiled but not bleached, and sold to be sliced and eaten with bread. It was not unknown for elder to be put into "chicken" sandwiches at seaside resorts. Cooked with a chicken and accompanied by a strong sage-and-onion stuffing, it took on the flavour and colour of the fowl, and was said to be almost indistinguishable from the real thing when cut and put between slices of bread!

For a period after the First World War and in the 1920s, Smith's provided "Tripe Suppers" for Ex-Servicemen's parties and similar events. The menu comprised tripe in an onion sauce, marrowfat peas and mashed potatoes, with plate apple pie to follow. Crockery was also provided, and the inclusive

Ground floor of the UCP restaurant, Bradshawgate, Bolton

cost was about a shilling a head.

Charlie Smith's had five or six hawkers - self employed men - who would go round the terraced streets ringing a handbell and selling tripe to the householders direct. The firm provided the carts and a set of scales for weighing out, but the men bought their own tripe. The slogan "It's in everybody's mouth - Smith's Tripe!" was painted on the sides of the handcarts and the delivery lorries.

Frank Smith, grandson of the founder, was born at 204 Bury Road, as was his father before him. His uncle Charles became an Alderman of the Borough, and was Chairman of the Markets Committee at one period. During election time local children would go around singing, "Vote for Charlie Smith, he gives you a pound of tripe!"

"One voting day," remembers a lady whose father ran a small farm, *"half a dozen women stood around my father's milk float, discussing the voting. My dad said he was voting for Charlie Smith, so he'd get a free tripe supper, and I told him, 'Dad, you've just lost about ten customers!'"*

Frank Smith remembers his grandfather as a portly man with a very bushy beard, somewhat resembling King Edward VII. Frank still has in his possession a pencil carrying the firm's motto: "It's in everybody's mouth - Smith's Tripe, absolutely the best!" and he believes these were given away to customers in the 1930s.

Voses shop and restaurant in Bradshawgate

Boltonians Talking Tripe

In 1894 John Mason took over a tripe shop at 238 Halliwell Road, which his wife and one of his daughters continued to run after his death. Mrs Smith of Farnworth has vivid memories of visiting her aunt and grandmother at the shop in the early years of this century.

"The counter was covered by a blue and white checked oilcloth. At one end was a copper boiler, probably heated by gas, for there was a sort of pipe at the back, and at the other end stood a large vinegar bottle. In the shop window there was a large marble slab with a ridge at the bottom for the liquid to run down and drain into a bucket placed underneath.

The window was tastefully dressed. The thick seam was at the front, with the jelly tripe behind, placed in layers, one piece on top of the other; behind this was the honeycomb. On one side were arranged the trotters and on the other the cowheels. The manifold, or 'black' tripe, and cowheel 'bits' on a plate, were at the back of the display.

The tripe came from Smiths at their Bury Road works. When I was about eight years old I used to take a basket and go there by tram. I'd say to the men, 'Auntie Nellie sent me for two cowheels and five pound o' tripe' (or whatever the order was for that day). Smith's tripe works seemed a very awesome place to me; it was dark inside, and very steamy, like a sort of cavern. There were big wooden barrels and thick wood boxes with bevelled edges and hand holes at each side for easy lifting. The men appeared very big and strange in the steamy atmosphere, and being only a small lass I found it a rather alarming but always a fascinating place.

One day the tripe was 'sticking', that is, not selling well. Auntie said to me: 'Go outside and shout "Tripe for sale!"' I was at the door before she told me she was only pulling my leg!

When weighing out the tripe, Grandma cut the thick seam into a wedge shape. She sold sheep's trotters for invalids, to give strength. These were cooked in milk with a spot of butter. Pigs' feet were bigger and coarser than trotters. Calf's-foot jelly, a light brown colour, was given to convalescents; people recovering from 'flu were advised to 'have a spoonful o' this'. Sometimes the cowheels had patches of fur left

on them; these were cut off and sold as cowheel 'bits' for twopence-halfpenny a pound. This was in the 1920s, when tripe was ninepence a pound and trotters were about three-halfpence each.

People 'believed' in tripe. Anyone with a 'queer tummy' could eat it with no ill effects.

On Saturday nights they cut up the tripe into little squares and put them on to wooden skewers. These were placed in the copper urn and warmed up and men coming out of the pubs used to buy the 'tripe-bits' to eat on the way home.

The next morning poor children of the neighbourhood would come knocking at the back door (being Sunday the front shop was closed) with the plea: ''Ave you any bree, missus?' Grandma would dole out the thick liquid and left-over scraps of tripe and cowheel from the previous day. Boiled up with cheap vegetables bought late at the Saturday market, this made a very acceptable soup, and for some children it was their only meal if their father had spent his wage or dole money on drink.

After Grandma died, my aunt took over the running of the shop, but she gradually went over to selling kitchenware and china. After the Second World War, as more regulations were brought in, and she was badgered by Public Health officials, she decided to close the business altogether."

* * * * *

Mrs Dean lived for about 15 years in a tripe shop on Harold Street, Halliwell. It had formerly been a baby linen shop, but when her father rented it from a friend (a mill manager), they converted it into a tripe shop.

"Father already had a job as a watchmaker in the town centre, so it was Mother who kept the shop. There was a sort of stable at the back; I think someone once kept a pony there. In the shop itself we had a table where customers could eat if they wished; there was always a supply of pickles and vinegar kept handy.

When I was about twelve years old I was sent to the UCP works for the tripe and cowheels; I also helped by cooking and cleaning, and on occasion was allowed to serve in the shop, which stayed open till eleven o'clock at night. We

Deansgate in the 1920s. The old Lower Nags Head pub is on the left and Voses shop (53 Deansgate) on the right, next to Burton's

sold the usual kinds of tripe, cowheels and trotters, and later on black puddings, savoury ducks, pies and teacakes."

After Mrs Dean's mother's health broke down the family moved to other premises and the tripe business was given up.

*   *   *   *   *

For a few years after the First World War, Mrs Hall worked for the UCP as a cook. She prepared tripe suppers with sausages and peas, onion sauce and steak and cowheel, which were sent out in enamel bowls and buckets to shops in Newport Street, Bradshawgate, Deansgate and Churchgate. Each shop cooked its own quota of potatoes.

Mr Hall was a driver for Voses for forty years, making deliveries to Bolton Royal Infirmary, Newlands Nursing Home, Haslam's Maternity Home and on to shops in Horwich, Whittle-le-Woods, Walton-le-Dale and Preston. Back in Bolton, he went over to the cattle market to pick up bellies for the works.

Mrs Hall: "I love tripe. All through the war it was ninepence a pound. We used to buy the 'pods', or broken trotters, and they were more tender than the trotters because they had broken in the cooking - and, of course, they were cheap!

I remember tripe on skewers and the bree. The shops used to have big canisters of bree on the counter, with a little light underneath so it was always kept hot. We used to go in Mrs Pilling's shop down Derby Street to buy half a pound of tripe. She would cut it up, put it on a skewer and drop it in the bree for a couple of minutes. Then she would lift the skewer out, take the tripe off and put it on a piece of white paper and give you the skewer to eat it with.

If we went to Blackpool on our holidays we would go to a tripe shop on Lytham Road. They had a little table with salt and vinegar on it, and me and my husband would sit there and have half a pound of tripe on plates. Then he'd say, 'Can you eat some more?' I'd say, 'Yes, we'll 'ave some more!' So we'd have two half pounds of tripe! Oh yes, I love tripe!

Trotters used to be cooked in milk, like mushrooms - they were recommended for invalids. You could eat them cold - I liked them cold - but the pods would be warmed up in a drop of milk. One part of the tripe, the thin end, was called 'invalid tripe'. There was the seam, honeycomb, manifold and the beef tripe, which was like a long, round 'wessan' (weasand). My husband said

Mr Haslam senior cleaning the windows of the Newport Street tripe shop

that in Preston they called manifold 'ladies' tripe' and I believe in Oldham they called it 'slutch' - it was dark coloured and wrinkled. I remember my sister once said, 'Oh, y'know Mrs So-an-So? Well, 'er face 'as gone just like manifold!'

My husband loved tripe and trotters but he didn't like cowheel. I loved it, but he wouldn't have it! My daughter also liked cowheel, so I used to cook steak and cowheel. My husband would cut a piece off and eat it raw, but he wouldn't have it cooked!

At one time the Halliwell family who had the Wheatsheaf shop (Voses, Newport Street) lived on the premises down at the works on Silverwell Lane. This was when they had horses, and Mr Halliwell was the horseman. When the firm did away with the horses and went on motors, the house was turned into offices. After Mrs Halliwell died, her daughter kept the Wheatsheaf shop on for a time."

*   *   *   *   *

Mr Haslam recalls living with his parents over the tripe shop on Newport Street for about six years until he was ten. Earlier, his mother had worked for a tripe shop in Tyldesley.

"Mother became Manageress of the Bradshawgate cafe and then the Newport Street shop about 1946-7. Steak and cowheel was a favourite dish with the patrons. Then there was the thick seam tripe, which was the 'face' piece - smooth, with plenty of fat; white honeycomb, 'wi' salt an' vinegar in every

A view down Newport Street with Voses shop next to the Wheatsheaf Hotel

'ole'; sheep's trotters done in milk, and pigs' feet, which were brown and would be eaten with Beetop sauce. Neatsfoot oil was purchased, too; some would rub it on their chests if they had a cold."

Mr Haslam himself served in the shop when he was eight years old. He recalls that orders for the following day were written out on 6"x4" tickets and taken to the works in the evening. The tripe was stored in ice and water in big porcelain vats until required.

"I remember UCP shops in Blackpool, facing the North Pier, and in Farnworth, near Longcauseway. I think the Bradshawgate cafe was the last to close in Bolton. A great saying of Mother's was: 'Keep to the UCP motto - never go into t'kitchen empty-handed!'"

* * * * *

Mr Hanson remembers how, as a young plasterer, he helped to put the mosaic under Voses' shop window on Churchgate corner; the background was white and the name was in black mosaic. He used to watch the tripe dressing on Bradshawgate and also recalls Charlie Smith's works.

"You could get tripe suppers for 9d or 10d, with tripe and onions, steak pudding and chips and so on. People used to go round the pubs with tripe on sticks; the cry was 'Put plenty alicker on!' Then there was rabbit pie or tripe in milk, with a parsley sauce.

On St Helens Road, at the bottom of Blackledge Street, there was a row of little low houses, and the second from the end was a tripe shop. Mrs Boardman was a typical red-faced Lancashire woman who sold black or 'rag' tripe. (Manifold was its proper name, but people used to call it rag tripe because it resembled a piece of old dishcloth.) Her husband Jack was a knocker-up; he charged 3d a week.

The UCP used to do funeral and wedding teas; there were a lot of funerals in the 1920s. Folk would set the coffin in the window so that people passing could look in at the corpse. It was quite a boast at one time - 'We kept 'er for a week!' There was also a special hearse for mother and child, in the days when women often died in childbirth. Incidentally, there was also a special 'funeral cake' - a large slab cake which was sold by the Maypole dairy on St Helens Road.

Children used to play at 'Jacks and Bobbers' or 'Pea-knuckle' with bones they got from trotters and pigs' feet..."

* * * * *

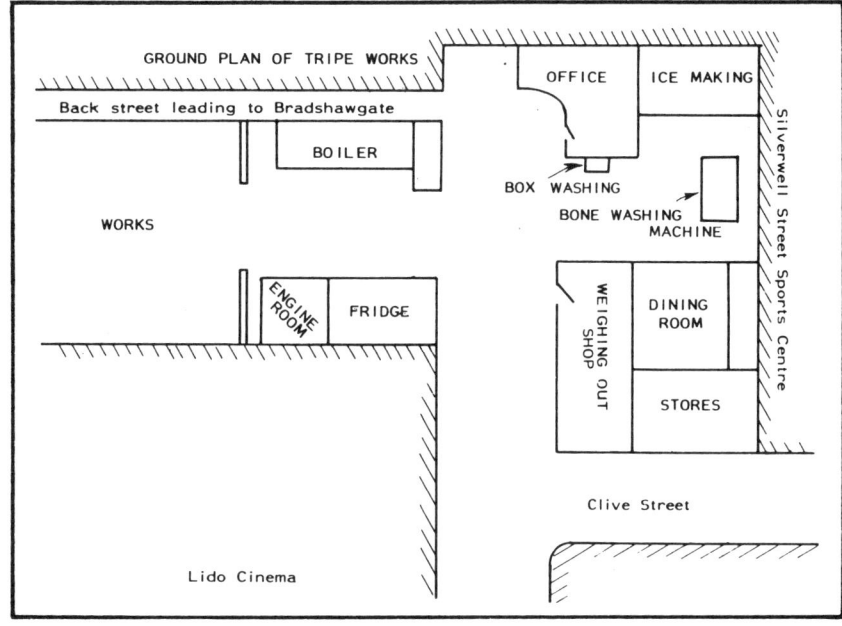

Plan of the Silverwell Lane tripe works

In 1935, at the age of 17, Bill Davies went to work for the UCP at their works behind Bradshawgate. The first of his many jobs was to prepare cow-heels and his wage was £1-7s.

Everyone was issued with clogs and bibbed overalls, but they made their own aprons out of sacking. Twice a week Bill had to take two bags of clogs down to Rogan's clog shop on Churchbank for mending. All drivers were inspected before going out on deliveries - they had to be smart and tidy in appearance.

When raw tripes were brought from the slaughterhouses, to-gether with four cowheels to each tripe (a 'set' of tripe), they were first hung on hooks. Then they were cut down, washed and given a preliminary cooking to help get the skin off by scraping. The tripes were then cooked properly. The older the animal was, the longer it took to cook, and an experienced cook was able to tell how old an animal was just by picking up the seam. Then they were placed in boilers for bleaching, after which they were put into iced water. When Bill worked on the night shift his last job was to lift the tripes out of the water, ready for delivering to the shops.

The night shift lasted from 6.00pm to 6.00am; day shifts started at 6.00am and continued until the day's work was completed, which might be four or five o'clock in the afternoon (hardly ever later than five) and then they worked on Sat-urday morning as well. Every-thing had to be scrubbed down thoroughly before going off the shift, the floors included, right down the back street outside

the works and on to Bradshaw-gate itself.

"Soon after I started work, about the year 1936, we held a cricket match on Bradshawgate. The night shift used to have their supper on top of the boiler, and some nights there would also be a Corporation gang working on the tramlines. They would have a vehicle fitted with arc lights, and on one particular night they threw out a challenge to the UCP men. We stood tripe boxes on the tramlines for wickets and play began. Our only spectator was a policeman on night beat."

Bill Davies was among the first to be called-up in 1939 - into the Militia, the "Hore Belisha men". Three months later war was declared and he was in the army for the duration. The first Christmas he was in the Forces, his wife was sent one week's wage, which is all they got from the UCP until he was demobbed!

* * * * *

Mrs Watson was manageress of the Bradshawgate UCP when it belonged to Voses. She was born in Southport in 1900 and when she was fifteen the family moved to Bolton. Her mother became Manageress of the Newport Street shop and cafe and it was whilst they were there that the Zeppelin raid on Bolton took place. The family and staff ran down into the cellars of the Wheatsheaf public house until the raid was over.

"As teenagers, we girls wore long plaits tied at the top and bottom with neat ribbon bows. Well, one day, rushing through the shop as usual (thinking myself very efficient), I felt a sudden tug at my hair. Turning round, I saw no-one behind me, but still felt my hair being pulled. Then I discovered that a long scoop, used for doling out the steak and cowheel, had somehow got itself caught in my plait and was swinging at my back, making an unusual ornament, much to the amusement of the customers and much to my embarrassment!"

The family moved on to other shops and cafes, notably the one on Deansgate, and finally to Bradshawgate, which boasted a fairly high class clientele, "commercial travellers and the like", although after the pubs shut there would be queues until closing time.

At the beginning of the 1939-45 War, the Territorials (whose Barracks lay just round the corner from the tripe works, on Silverwell Street) were treated to a Farewell Supper by the UCP. This took place when the shop had closed, after 11.00pm. The following morning, as the soldiers passed before the shop on their way to the station, the UCP staff assembled to watch them go. Their officer called out: "Eyes left!" and to a man the soldiers saluted the girls as they marched past. There were few dry eyes that day.

"We sold tripe and onions, tripe on a skewer, tripe bits (about a quarter, with a small piece of seam on top) and dripping - every customer could take half a pound of dripping with their tripe, if they wanted it.

Behind the counter there was bree on a hotplate. Hot steak and cowheel was tenpence and

UCP staff outing on Bradshawgate in the 1960s. In the group are Mrs Scholes (manageress) and her daughter Vera (supervisor) and Olive Walker

a shilling, and for the same price you could have a plate of mashed potato, sausage and peas, or sausage and a quarter of tripe, with an onion sauce poured over it."

Mrs Watson had to give up work soon after the beginning of the war; her sister worked for 48 years for the UCP.

* * * * *

Joan Taylor started work as a tripedresser for the UCP at the age of 14. Arthur and Stanley Hill were the Directors then, and after Smith's tripe works closed Charlie Smith came into the firm. Joan's fellow workers were Mr Greenhalgh, who was

the foreman until he retired and was succeeded by John Morris; John's brother Harry, Bill Davies, Beattie and Annie Thompson; sisters Maggie, Annie and Polly Cummings; Dick Fulger, Derek Whittle the boilerman; Mercy Nuttall; Nora Davies and her husband Jimmy; Tommy Jolly and his two sons Herbert and Reggie; Peter Thompson in the weighing-out shop; Arthur and Kenny Evans and little Billy Barnes, known simply as "t'child".

"Work was very cold in winter, especially on our feet, but even though we worked in icy water we never got chapped hands because the grease clung to the skin. We wore aprons made from the sacks which the tripes came in - washed out first, naturally! There were always a lot of cats about the works, to keep the rats and mice down.

Maggie Cummings once told me about the Zeppelin raid on Bolton. There was a little chapel at the back of the Lido cinema on Bradshawgate and the dead were carried into the church hall. Maggie was a cook at that time and often worked on her own at night."

Joan's favourite recipe is well-liked in Bolton: cut up half a pound of stewing steak and cook slowly with carrots, barley and half a cowheel, chopped up. About half an hour before the end of cooking time, put a thick suet crust on top. "It sticks to your ribs in winter!"

* * * * *

William Evans began as an apprentice dresser at the Bolton UCP in 1954, and remembers particularly Polly and Annie

Bill Evans, Annie Cummings, Beattie Thompson, and Polly Cummings outside the Silverwell Lane tripe works

Cummings – *"who practically ran the place between them!"*

The foreman was John Morris; Arthur Winward was the trotter and cowheel cook, who later went to live in Blackpool. There were also Brian Huddle, Jimmy Lunt, Bill Fernside and Dick Smith, who took over from Bill Fernside when he left. The boiler man was Jim Davies.

"The stomachs were collected from the slaughterhouse on Weston Street, brought to the works and classed according to age and weight. We used very sharp knives when cleaning the tripes, and there were frequent accidents, such as cut hands and arms.

The tripedressing was done in becks; the skin had to be re-moved from the stomach in the water, and the skill was to leave as much fat (seam) on the belly as possible.

After cooking, trotters were pared, that is, the fur and hooves were taken off. The fur was collected and put into a device which compressed it so that water and oil was extracted; the oil was then taken off the surface of the water. Cowheels were cooked in the same way, but classed before cooking. The age was checked by feeling each heel at the bone, in order to judge the cooking time. There was also a machine for washing bones.

Upstairs, above the boiler, hooves were cooked and bagged ready to be sent off to the glue factory. Ice was also made on the premises and sold to

UCP Chef Fred Laycock showing off his culinary skills outside the restaurant on Bradshawgate, Bolton. The manageress, Mrs Scholes, is standing behind him

shops. The sacks in which the tripes arrived were washed, dried and sold. Nothing was wasted!"

* * * * *

Mr Arthur Strand comments: *"Although tripe sales in general were highest in summer, Bolton also managed high sales in winter because tripe was eaten cooked with onions. I have been told that local tripe-dressers used to tour the public houses, selling hot tripe served on hand-made wooden skewers.*

Cowheel was likewise in great demand. This was cooked with meat to make it go further and feed a whole family. It was also a tradition in the Bolton area to have steak and cowheel pie on New Year's Eve.

The tripe industry – not a very clean, pleasant or glamorous one – grew too expensive and, with an increase in Public Health regulations, it became too much trouble for the majority of family-run businesses to continue in operation. As older members of the family retired or passed on, the younger ones simply let the business go or were taken over by larger concerns.

Some years ago I had a market stall in Burnley, where we sold a large amount of tripe which was eaten at the stall. On Saturdays we could easily sell around a thousand plates of tripe, soaking up a gallon of vinegar!"

* * * * *

Mrs Crompton *"closed the last tripe shop in Bolton".* This was Betty's Tripe Shop at 95 Tonge Moor Road, near the Starkie Arms.

"We sold various kinds of tripe, as well as elder, pigs' feet, savoury ducks, pickled herrings and so on; also donkey stones and a few grocery items. The tripe was delivered daily from the UCP. During hot weather – the best weather for selling tripe – it was sometimes de-livered twice a day.

The tripe was laid out in the window bottom on a sloping marble slab which had a hole

Betty's Tripe Shop, Tonge Moor Road, Bolton. Mrs Young, the lady in the shawl, had been coming to the shop since she was a little girl, when all they sold were tripe products, donkey stones and firewood! Mrs Young was in her nineties when she died.

halfway along a ridge at the base. This was to allow the excess water in which the tripe had been kept to drain off. Customers would say, 'Shake t' watter off - watter weighs 'eavy!'"

Betty's tripe shop, which was among the last to operate purely as a tripe shop, finally closed its doors about 1979.

* * * * *

Mr Walkden recalls a small works which existed at the corner of High Street and was run by Mr and Mrs Jenkinson, who, he believes, had formerly been on the professional stage, possibly with a song-and-dance act.

"They had a son called Neville who moved to Southport in 1922, but I remember most a girl called Bertha. She lived with the family, although I don't think she was any relation. Bertha had a soft spot for me and often slipped me tripe bits

in paper on the sly, whenever the opportunity arose. I was about ten years old at the time!

It was only a small place, and the works was at the back. The Jenkinsons provided meals such as tripe and onions, and sold tripe products and chitterlings."

* * * * *

Mr Crompton recalls a man going round the streets with a handcart, calling out: "Block salt! Tripe bits on a skewer!" There was also a man named Young who lived on Bury Road. He boiled tripe on the river bank, behind a wooden fence on the corner of Kestor Street.

* * * * *

A gentleman now in his eighties remembers taking tea every Monday at the Bank Street cafe: *"It was a common sight to see men and women eating tripe out of paper; I was once told it sobers you up! Lawrence Taylor,*

who had a shop up Tonge Moor (his son was MP for Bolton some years back), always put cowheel in his meat pies. He was a Westhoughton man, with a strong Lanky accent. Every New Year's Eve he'd send a pork pie round, and with it a note - 'For eytin'!"

* * * * *

"After an evening spent at the Grand," recalls an elderly lady, *"we used to call at Voses on Churchgate and buy a pennorth o' tripe bits in paper. Then we'd walk along Kay Street, on our way home to Halliwell, eating the tripe and discussing the entertainment!"*

* * * * *

When his wife was pregnant, a young man was advised by his father: *"Get some neatsfoot oil to rub on 'er stomach. It'll prevent stretch marks!"*

* * * * *

Part 5

Tripe - Past, Present and Future

In the 1950s the towns and cities of the industrial North were still served by individuals in small shops, though many of these shops were owned by, or bought their products from, the larger combines. Ten years on, however, these places were closing down at a rapid rate, or else changing over to other lines. (One Bolton shop was transformed into a "Doggy Beauty Salon"!) Modern cafes and restaurants were still being opened well into the 1960s, but most of the retail trade was by then being carried on through market stalls or butchers' shops.

One of the last of the little shops is the Tripe Shop on Melbourne Street, Stalybridge, run by Mrs Marion Wilde, who buys her products from Parry Scragg Ltd. The prestigious UCP restaurants have also closed, the premises being given over to products unconnected with tripe.

What have we gained or lost by these changes? And how has the trade benefitted, if at all?

The gain has been in greater efficiency. Because of centralised control, businesses are more cost effective, especially from the point of view of administration. With the advent of refrigerated vans and motorways, goods are delivered much farther afield. Better marketing

is also possible, although the modern techniques available are not always fully exploited.

On the debit side, we have lost a lot of individuality. The larger combines cannot offer the same kind of personal service as formerly given. Older people preferred the little shops, which were, in the words of one devotee, "Very friendly places, warm and homely." The trade then was more of a public service than a business.

Shop closures were bound to affect custom to a large extent. Folk went to the tripe shop specifically to buy tripe or other offal products, whereas today, "You're lucky if you see any at all!" Other than on town centre market stalls, some few pieces of tripe might be found languishing on a tray in a butcher's window, in direct competition with a host of other meats on display there. Small wonder, then, that sales are not what they were. Tripe itself, some of the older generation assert, is "not what it was" - meaning that it is not as flavoursome. Is this indeed the case?

The present trade is overshadowed by the emergence of competitive alternative food, such as frozen and canned goods and takeaways. Many production workers take their

The Tripe Shop on Melbourne Street, Stalybridge, in 1988

mid-day meals in works' canteens, others partake of the modern "bar snack", whilst their offspring have the advantage of cooked school lunches.

Add to this the general decline in the preparation of older traditional dishes, and the fact that tripe these days has something of a "poor" image, smacking of the "clogs and shawl era" which many prefer to forget, and you have the principal causes of diminution in this industry.

What of the future? Obviously tripe is still a good buy – what seems to be needed is more and better publicity. Instruction on how to cook and serve various tripe dishes would not come amiss. Teachers of Home Economics could help by taking a more positive attitude towards the product, by demonstrating simple dishes and showing how easily they can be prepared, from the well-known tripe and onions to a whole range of foreign or unusual concoctions.

Tripe can be used as a partial substitute for the meat content in many dishes, with the resulting meal being palatable and appreciated by the menfolk as a change from the usual menu. (This might be looking at the idea with rather TOO much optimism – the conservatism of most males, in their eating habits especially, is renowned!)

There could be improved packaging and display of the product to make the selling of tripe more attractive – posters and recipe cards in bright, colourful and bold lettering. Could not some enterprising tripedresser put out a series of illustrated menu and recipe

Well designed recipe card issued by the UCP in the 1980s

cards, showing how tripe can be used as a starter or in main course dishes? Judging by the number of recipes I have collected, there seems no lack of possibilities for such an undertaking!

Although it is a traditional Lancashire food, many modern Lancastrians have never actually tasted tripe and turn up their noses at the thought of eating it. As for trotters, they are hardly used at all in today's cuisine, being considered "too fiddly" – yet they are quite delicious when cooked slowly on a gentle heat, in the old way.

Tripe has long been a target for comedians, but as one tripedresser remarked, "People

think tripe is funny for some reason – for folk in the trade I can assure you it is a very serious matter indeed!"

A final note of optimism. R Heys & Sons was first established in Leeds in 1953 and six years later they moved to Dewsbury. Mrs Heys gives the following reasons for current difficulties in the trade:

1 Staffing problems – it is not a very exciting or pleasant job to be in.

2 A general decline in meat eating.

3 Supermarkets taking business from traditional markets and town centre shops.

4 Tripedressing is still a "cottage industry" and so it is not promoted efficiently enough.

Whatever problems there are, however, the Heys family firm is thriving, to the extent that they have now opened shops in Wakefield and Batley, profiting from television programmes, newspaper advertising and the publication of a recipe booklet.

The Heys slogan – "Don't talk tripe – EAT it!" – sums up, with typical Northern wit, the message contained in these pages!

****
For a current list of local history publications please send a stamped addressed envelope to Neil Richardson, 375 Chorley Rd, Swinton, Manchester M27 2AY
****

UCP tripe shop on Topping Street, Blackpool, in 1988

Part 6
Tripe Recipes

Traditional

Tripe can produce any number of tasty dishes to suit any time of the year, but it is especially popular during the summer months. Cold tripe seasoned with salt, pepper and vinegar and served with salad is a delicious and ideal food. However, tripe is in season all the year round, and as reliable and desirable in January as in August.

To keep tripe at its best, place it in fresh cold water in a cool place. DON'T allow it to dry out. Run cold water over it before use.

The following are the most generally prepared recipes here in the North. (All are for 3-4 persons, unless stated otherwise)

TRIPE AND ONIONS
Here are three variations on a theme, from Lancashire, Yorkshire and Wales!

LANCASHIRE:
2 Spanish onions	½ pint milk
1½lb pre-cooked tripe	seasoning
1 oz flour	pinch nutmeg
1 oz butter	toast

1. Peel the onions and stew them with the tripe, just covered with water, until tender.
2. Drain, reserving half the pourings. Cut the tripe into pieces; chop the onions.
3. Melt the butter in a heat-proof dish and mix in the flour; slowly add the tripe and onion pourings.
4. Stir until boiling, add the milk, seasoning, tripe and onions, and simmer for 10 to 15 minutes.
5. Serve with toast. For four people.

YORKSHIRE:
2 lb dressed tripe	1 oz butter
1 lb sliced onions	1 oz flour
salt and pepper	2 tablespoons grated
½ pint each milk & water	cheese

1. Cut the tripe into bite-sized pieces and put into a saucepan with the onions, milk and water; season to taste.
2. Bring to the boil, cover and simmer gently for an hour, or until the tripe is tender.
3. Mix the butter and flour together, and when all the flour is absorbed break into small pieces and put into the tripe, stirring all the time until the liquid thickens.
4. Transfer to an ovenproof dish, sprinkle grated cheese over the top and brown, either in the oven or under a hot grill. Serves 4.

WALES:
1 lb tripe	1 oz butter
1 medium sized onion	1½ pints milk & water
1 oz flour	salt and pepper

1. Cut the prepared tripe into 2" squares, skin and dice the onion; season to taste.
2. Simmer the tripe and onion in the milk and water for 1 hour, until the tripe is tender.
3. Melt the butter in another saucepan and work in the flour; stir in a little stock from the tripe. Return the flour mixture to the main saucepan. Stir well and bring back to the boil.
4. Cook gently for 2-3 minutes. Serve hot with boiled Gower potatoes and creamed button mushrooms. Serves 3-4

* * * * *

Here are some more popular Northern dishes...

STUFFED TRIPE
A large piece of tripe is filled with a mixture composed of breadcrumbs, chopped bacon, chopped onion, some sage and seasoning. The edges are well secured, then the whole is placed into a greased baking tin and covered by strips of bacon. This is then cooked in the oven for about an hour.

HUDDERSFIELD TRIPE
Tripe is thinly sliced and covered with sliced onions which have been marinated in vinegar, salt and pepper. This is eaten as it is, without cooking.

TRIPE PLOT
A nourishing invalid dish.
½ lb pre-cooked tripe	½ teacup milk
1 egg (beaten up)	pepper and salt
parsley	toast (optional)

1. Cut the tripe into very small pieces and place into a casserole dish.
2. Add the milk and season to taste. Simmer for 5 minutes.
3. Transfer the tripe into a warm dish. Add the beaten egg to the liquor in the casserole, then stir over a low heat until the sauce thickens. (NB: Do not allow the heat to reach boiling point.)
4. Pour the sauce over the tripe, garnish with parsley and serve, with toast if required.

* * * * *

As well as tripe, we have, of course, a fondness for cowheel here in the North, and as a Boltonian I must not omit trotters. So here are some recipes using these products...

COWHEEL STEW
1 cowheel	1 teaspoon vinegar
1 large onion	1 oz butter
1 bouquet garni	2 tablesp cornflour
1 bayleaf	pepper & salt to taste
mustard (optional)	parsley (optional)

1. Scald, clean and split the heel, put into a large saucepan, with the onion, bouquet garni, bayleaf and vinegar.
2. Bring almost to the boil, then let simmer gently for 4 hours.
3. Empty the contents into a basin, put the saucepan back on the heat and melt the butter in it, adding next the flour and seasoning. Next blend in the cowheel gravy and leave to cook for some minutes.
4. Meanwhile, bone the cowheel and cut up the meat into neat pieces; slice the cooked onion and add to the meat.
5. Pour the sauce over the meat mixture, serve with mashed potatoes and garnish with parsley. Mustard may be served with the dish, if liked.

COWHEEL BRAWN
1 cowheel	chopped cooked bacon (about 2 oz)
1 onion	pepper, salt

1. Wash cowheel and stew very slowly, preferably overnight, with the onion.
2. Take out the bones and chop the meat very finely.
3. Add the cooked, chopped bacon and salt and pepper to taste.
4. Pack it into a pudding basin, with a saucer on top to weight it, if necessary.
5. When cold and set it may be sliced up thinly and served with mustard, or mixed pickles and bread and butter.

BATTERED TROTTERS
4 sheep's trotters	3 or 4 celery stalks
1 onion	pepper, salt, water
½ lb carrots	batter

1. Stew trotters very slowly (can take all day!) in enough water to cover.
2. Meantime, make a fairly thick batter and leave to stand until required.
3. Take trotters from heat and bone them. Dip into batter (thinned down with juice from trotter boiling; a few spoonfuls is enough).
4. Fry the battered trotters. Boil down the trotter juice and serve as a gravy with the cooked meat and vegetables.

New and Unusual Dishes

TRIPE WITH LEMON

1 lb tripe, cut into 1" squares
2 large onions
¼ lb mushrooms
¾ pint chicken stock
cayenne pepper
1 tablespoon lemon juice

2 tablespoons butter
2 tablespoons flour
2 tablesp fresh cream
seasoning

1. Fry onion with mushrooms until softened, in melted butter.
2. Add flour and cook for a further 2 minutes, then add the chicken stock and bring to the boil.
3. Add the lemon juice, tripe and a pinch of cayenne pepper. Cook for 40 minutes on a low heat.
4. Just before serving add the fresh cream. Serve on a bed of boiled rice, and decorate with asparagus tips.

TRIPE RISSOLES

1 finely chopped onion
2 large potatoes, mashed
1 lb cooked, minced tripe
flour, fresh breadcrumbs

1 egg, beaten up
anchovy essence
seasoning

1. Fry onion in a little fat.
2. Add to mashed potatoes (cold), anchovy essence and minced tripe.
3. Mould into shapes, and coat in egg and breadcrumbs, as for meat rissoles.
4. Fry in fat as for meat rissoles.
Makes about 8.

NB: If fried from frozen state, they tend to hold their shape better.

TRIPE PATE

½ lb cooked tripe
3 oz cream cheese
1 chopped onion

2 oz butter
tomato puree
cayenne pepper, parsley

1. Fry onion in a knob of butter. Add shredded, cooked tripe, cook for 3 minutes.
2. Place in liquidiser with cream cheese, butter, tomato puree and seasoning.
3. When well blended turn into a dish and cool for at least half an hour.
4. Garnish with parsley. Serve with fingers of toast and water biscuits.

TRIPE AS AN HORS D'OEUVRE

½ lb ready cooked tripe (cut into 1" squares)
French dressing (made of oil, vinegar, mustard, sugar, seasoning): chopped chives, etc.

1. Place tripe in an hors d'oeuvres dish, coat with French dressing, and sprinkle with chopped chives or parsley.
2. Serve, accompanied by other cocktail dishes, such as egg mayonnaise, tomato salad, cocktail onions, cheese dip, etc. (Don't forget the cocktail sticks!)

TRIPE A L'ITALIENNE

1 lb dressed tripe, cut into 1" squares
14 oz tin tomatoes   4 oz mushrooms, sliced
seasoning; oregano or marjoram
1 large onion, diced   oil, flour (2 tablesp)

1. Fry onions and mushrooms in oil (or butter, if preferred).
2. Add flour, heat up for a couple of minutes.

3. Add tomatoes and tripe and seasoning; simmer for half an hour.
4. Serve with buttered noodles. (New potatoes make an acceptable accompaniment instead of noodles.)

MOULDED TRIPE

1 lb tripe
¾ pint water

½ cowheel
pepper, salt

1. Cut up the cowheel, season well and cover with water; simmer until tender (about 2 hours). Remove bones, chop cowheel meat finely.
2. Cut tripe into strips, add to the liquid, simmer for 10 minutes.
3. Fill a rinsed mould with alternate layers of cowheel and tripe; pour enough hot liquid over to cover.
4. Leave till cold. Turn out and decorate with parsley.

TRIPE HOT POT

1 lb pre-cooked tripe
2 lb potatoes
1 tablesp beef dripping
3 tomatoes

1 lb onions
stock
1 oz flour
salt and pepper

1. Wipe the tripe, cut up and dip in seasoned flour.
2. Peel potatoes and onions, and cut into slices; slice tomatoes.
3. Fill a greased hot-pot dish with alternate layers of vegetables and tripe, starting and finishing with potatoes and seasoning each layer.
4. Pour in stock to halfway up the dish, dot top with dripping, cover with a lid.
5. Bake for 1½ hours at gas mark 5 or 375°F, taking off the lid for the last 15 minutes to brown the potatoes.

TRIPE SOUP

½ lb pre-cooked tripe
1 onion
½ oz flour

1 oz butter
½ pint milk
½ pint water   seasoning

1. Peel and chop onion, cook in water until tender.
2. Cut up tripe into tiny pieces, add to the onion and cook for 10 minutes.
3. In another pan melt the butter, add flour, cook for a few seconds. Add liquor from tripe and onion, stirring all the time until it thickens.
4. Add tripe and onions, milk and season to taste. (Also 1 beef stock cube if desired.) Bring slowly to boil and serve. Serve in warm soup bowls garnished with toast.

BEEF AND COWHEEL PASTY

Cowheel
pepper, salt
3 oz margarine or lard

¼ lb shin beef
6 oz flour
milk

1. Cut up cowheel and meat, just cover with water, season and simmer until tender (about 3 hours or 30 minutes in a pressure cooker).
2. Strain, remove bones and chop or mince the meat finely. Moisten with some of the liquor.
3. Add salt to the flour, rub in the fat and mix to a soft dough with cold water. Divide into two equal parts.
4. Line an oven-proof plate with one half of the pastry, spread meat over and cover with remaining piece of pastry, rolled out slightly larger than the plate, but without stretching.
5. Trim and decorate the edge of the pastry, make a hole in the centre. Brush with milk or egg. Bake for 30 minutes in a moderate oven, gas No.8 or 400°F. Serve hot or cold. Serves 2.

TRIPE WIGGLE

1 lb tripe   ½ oz butter or marg.
½ pint white sauce (½ oz each of butter,
cornflour; ½ pt milk, salt and pepper)
4oz shrimps or prawns   seasoning, pinch of mace
parsley, squeeze of lemon juice
lemon slices to garnish

1. Gently fry the tripe in butter for 5 minutes (cut into bite-size pieces)
2. Make white sauce
3. Add tripe and prawns to the sauce, check seasoning, add mace and lemon juice. Cook gently for 3 minutes. Serve, garnished with parsley and lemon slices.

     Serves 2, or makes a delicious starter for a meal serving 4-6, in individual dishes.

TRIPE ROLL

1½ lb tripe   nutmeg
4 large potatoes   milk
1 tblsp chopped parsley   flour for dusting
1 onion   salad oil
2 cups breadcrumbs   3-4 slices fat bacon
2 oz cooked ham   a little tomato ketchup
seasoning

1. Select a piece of tripe in one piece, shaped so that it can be rolled. Cook until tender.
2. Boil and mash potatoes, add to them parsley, chopped onion, breadcrumbs, finely chopped ham, pepper, salt, a pinch nutmeg. Moisten with milk.
3. Spread tripe with potato mixture, roll tightly and tie with string. Dust with flour, brush with oil and again dust with flour.
4. Lay strips of bacon across, place in baking tin. Bake for 1 hour at gas No.4. Serves 3-4. (Serve with hot ketchup.)

TRIPE AND PRAWN COCKTAIL SAUCE
An unusual starter

Pre-cooked seam tripe   fresh cream
mayonnaise   vinegar
tomato ketchup

1. Add mayonnaise to tomato ketchup (quantities one-to-one).
2. Add a teaspoon or two of fresh cream and a little vinegar to make the cocktail sauce.
3. Stir well, and pour mixture over diced (prawn size) cubes of seam tripe.

TRIPE A LA MODE DE CAEN

2lb pre-cooked tripe   2 carrots
1 cowheel   2-3 onions
3 leeks   3 cloves
a spring of thyme   a bayleaf
seasoning, water or cider

1. Cut cowheel and tripe into small pieces; prepare and slice the vegetables.
2. Into a deep casserole put a layer of vegetables, with the cloves and herbs.
3. Add cowheel and tripe, salt and pepper. Cover with a layer of vegetables, continuing thus until all ingredients are used up, ending with sliced leeks.
4. Pour in enough water or cider to come half-way up the sides of the casserole.
5. Put on lid and cook slowly in a moderate oven (gas mark 4 or 350°F) for 3-4 hours, until all ingredients are cooked through.
6. To serve: remove bones of the cowheel, and colour liquid with a little brown sugar, if liked.

TRIPE IN CELERY SAUCE
A quick meal

1 lb pre-cooked tripe   ½ oz flour
Can of cream of celery soup   a little milk

1. Pour soup into a pan, bring almost to boiling point.
2. Blend flour with a little milk; add gradually to the soup, stirring until it thickens.

3. Cut tripe into suitable pieces and simmer in the sauce for approximately 10 minutes.
4. Place on a serving dish, with a border of mashed potatoes and peas, or grilled tomato. (Serves 2)

TRIPE SALAD
A summer dish

1 lb pre-cooked tripe   spring onions
cold, cooked potatoes   seasoning
1 beetroot   chopped parsley
mayonnaise or salad dressing

1. Dice potatoes, add onions (finely chopped), and mix with enough salad dressing to coat; arrange on a dish.
2. Cut tripe into small pieces and heap on to the potato mixture; coat with salad dressing.
3. Slice the beetroot and arrange around the dish. Sprinkle with chopped parsley.
4. Serve very cold.

BATTERED TRIPE
Excellent with chips

Pre-cooked tripe   batter mix

1. Cut flat pieces of tripe into handy-size squares and dab dry.
2. Dip into thick batter mix and deep fry until golden brown.

SAVOURY TRIPE
A traditional recipe

1½ lbs pre-cooked tripe   ¼ lb mushrooms
1 pt stock or water   2 tablesp breadcrumbs
½ lb tomatoes   1½ oz beef dripping
1 tablespoon flour   grated cheese
seasoning

1. Wipe tomatoes, peel and wash the mushrooms; cut both into suitable pieces.
2. Melt dripping in a pan and fry the above for a few minutes; lift out and keep hot.
3. Add flour to the fat in the pan and allow to brown slightly. Pour in stock or water, stir until boiling. Season.
4. Cut tripe into neat pieces and lay in a greased casserole dish.
5. Cover with mushrooms and tomatoes, then pour sauce over. Sprinkle with breadcrumbs and grated cheese.
6. Cook until brown in a moderate oven, for about half an hour. Serve with fried or roasted potatoes.

FRIED TRIPE AND BACON

1 lb pre-cooked tripe   ¼ pint water
½ lb bacon rashers   1 dessert sp tomato
½ oz flour   pepper, salt   ketchup

1. Fry bacon rashers.
2. Fry sliced tripe in the bacon fat until golden brown
3. Sprinkle flour into the fat left in the pan, stirring for a couple of minutes.
4. Add water, ketchup and seasoning. When hot and thick pour over the tripe and bacon. Serve with mashed potatoes.

GRILLED TRIPE
For weight watchers

1 lb pre-cooked tripe
1 tablespoon vinegar or lemon juice
1 tablespoon finely-chopped parsley
2 tablespoon melted butter
1 tablespoon chopped onion
seasoning   browned breadcrumbs

1. Mix together parsley, onion, vinegar, butter and seasoning.
2. Wipe tripe and cut into bite-sized pieces, dip into savoury mixture and coat with breadcrumbs.
3. Brown under a very hot grill for 5 minutes each side. (Serves 2)

TRIPE CASSEROLE

Winter warmer

$1\frac{1}{2}$ lb pre-cooked tripe	4 oz mushrooms
2 tablesp vinegar	1 onion
1 pint water	1 tablesp plain flour
1 can peas or tomatoes	pepper, salt

1. Cut tripe into pieces about 2" square, soak in vinegar and water for 30 minutes.
2. Peel and slice mushrooms, chop onion.
3. Lightly fry tripe in a little fat, add mushrooms and onion. Remove from pan and add flour, pepper and salt. Stir until sauce is smooth; pour in vinegar and water and bring to boil.
4. Add peas or tomatoes, mushrooms, onions and tripe; turn the mixture into a fire-proof dish.
5. Bake in a moderately hot oven, gas No.7 or 425°F, for $\frac{3}{4}$ hour.

FRENCH PIQUANTE

$2\frac{1}{2}$ lbs tripe	$\frac{1}{2}$ lb sliced carrots
$1\frac{1}{2}$ oz butter	$\frac{1}{4}$ teaspoon thyme
3 onions	2 cloves garlic (optional)
1 bayleaf	2 tbsp chopped parsley
1 tbsp vinegar (or lemon)	
$1\frac{1}{4}$ oz plain flour	5 fl oz boiling water

1. Cut tripe into strips, $2\frac{1}{2}$"x$\frac{1}{2}$", Melt butter in saucepan.
2. Saute chopped onion, garlic and thinly sliced carrot until light brown.
3. Add chopped parsley, thyme, bayleaf and lemon juice or vinegar.
4. Simmer for 5 minutes. Sprinkle flour on to mixture and stir well.
5. Add boiling water, add tripe and check seasoning.
6. Cook for 10-12 minutes, stirring occasionally. Turn out into serving dish.
7. Serve with creamed potatoes, green peas, sliced beans or carrot fingers. (Serves 6)

SPANISH TRIPE

$2\frac{1}{2}$ lb cooked tripe	1 large onion
$\frac{1}{4}$ teaspoon salt	2 tbsp chopped parsley
$\frac{1}{2}$ teaspoon sugar	3 oz chopped celery
1 clove garlic	5 oz tomato puree
6 oz patna rice	2 oz cooked chopped mushrooms
1 teaspoon Worcester sauce	
pinch cayenne	2 oz cooked chopped ham and bacon

1. Boil rice in salted water until tender (12-15 minutes). Wash well under cold running water and leave to drain; re-heat by pouring boiling water through strainer; put into serving dish, leave in cool oven until required.
2. Put chopped onion and celery into a pan, with sufficient water to cover. Add salt, cook until tender.
3. Add garlic, sugar, tomato puree, cayenne pepper, Worcester sauce, salt, pepper and half the parsley. Cook on a low heat for 5 minutes.
4. Add tripe (cut into 1" squares), cooked ham and mushrooms, and re-heat to serving temperature.
5. Put prepared rice into a shallow dish to form a border, add contents of pan into the centre. Decorate with remainder of parsley. (Serves 6)

HUNGARIAN TRIPE

2 lbs tripe	2 oz butter, marg or oil
$\frac{1}{2}$ teaspoon salt	1 level tbsp paprika
1 rounded tablespoon plain flour	
3-4 medium to small onions	4 oz mushrooms
1 chicken stock cube (or $\frac{1}{2}$ lb cooked cowheel)	
2 level tbsp tomato puree	$\frac{1}{2}$ pint milk
pinch of marjoram or bouquet garni	

1. Cut tripe into $\frac{1}{2}$" squares. Wash and slice mushrooms, finely chop onion.
2. Pre-heat cooker to 275°F (gas No.1)
3. Saute finely chopped onion in butter or oil; cook gently until golden.
4. Add more fat to pan and when hot add sliced mushrooms, saute for 2-3 minutes; add paprika; cook for a further 2-3 minutes. Add flour, cook for another 4 minutes, stirring to avoid burning. (This should be cooked over a low heat.)
5. Slowly blend in the milk to form a thick sauce. Add stock cube, tripe and remaining ingredients.
6. Place in a covered casserole dish and cook on the middle shelf of the oven for approx two hours. (Serves 6)

* * * * *

Recipes from Abroad

China

PIG TRIPE SOUP

1 lb prepared tripe	$\frac{3}{4}$ level teasp sugar
coarse salt	vinegar
1 oz dried bean curd, softened in water	
1 can gingko, drained (optional)	
8 fluid oz (1 cup) pale dry sherry	
3 oz ($\frac{1}{2}$ cup) skinned unsalted peanuts (optional)	
2 teasp light soy sauce	$1\frac{1}{2}$ level teasp salt
$\frac{1}{2}$ level teasp MSG (monosodium glutamate)	

1. Rinse the tripe thoroughly under cold water.
2. Slice it into strips, $\frac{1}{2}$"x2".
3. Simmer in $1\frac{1}{4}$ pints water, with sherry, soy sauce, seasonings and softened bean curd, cut into strips like the tripe, adding gingko and peanuts if liked.
4. Stew for about $2\frac{1}{2}$ hours, or until very tender.

PIG'S FOOT JELLY

3 lbs pigs feet (3 or 4), split in half	
2 level teasp salt	2 tbsp light soy sauce
$\frac{1}{2}$ level teasp sugar	$\frac{3}{4}$ level teasp MSG
$\frac{3}{4}$ level teasp wild pepper, crushed	
$\frac{1}{2}$ lb very lean pork, minced	

1. Rinse the feet in cold water.
2. Stew for about $2\frac{3}{4}$ hours in $1\frac{1}{2}$ pints water with salt, soy sauce, sugar and crushed wild pepper, until the bones come loose. Remove bones.
3. Add MSG and another $\frac{1}{4}$ pint water; bring to the boil and reduce the heat.
4. Stir in the minced pork and continue to stir until the pork is cooked (about 5 minutes).
5. Pour the mixture into a straight-sided bowl and smooth out.
6. Leave it to cool until set, then unmould it and cut into very thin slices.

This is excellent served with ribbon rolls, or Pinwheels and wild pepper mix. (See any Chinese cookbook) After the jelly, serve a little dish of cabbage and some rice; it is enough!

* * * * *

France

TRIPE AND POTATO TERRINE

1 pig's foot, large bone removed, split, covered with cold water for 10 minutes, drained and rinsed.
$1\frac{1}{2}$ lb beef tripe, cut into approx 2" squares
8 oz olives, green or black, parboiled for 1 minute, then drained.
2 teasp crumbled thyme (or mixed dried herbs)
1 heaped tablesp finely chopped garlic
1 heaped tablesp finely chopped parsley
3/4 bayleaves; salt; water; flour for dougn
$2\frac{1}{2}$ lb potatoes, cut into $\frac{1}{4}$" slices
(+ any leftover meat roasting juices)

1. In the bottom of a quart-sized casserole (earthenware preferable) put pig's foot and enough pieces of tripe to line.
2. Sprinkle over this the olives, the herb/garlic mix, 1 bayleaf and some salt.
3. Add a layer of sliced potatoes, a layer of tripe, then more seasoning and herbs, and so on, finishing with a layer of potatoes.
4. Press the surface to pack the contents slightly, pour on enough boiling water to cover.
5. Make a flour and water dough, roll out to a ribbon with the hands, and place around the edges of the dish; this is to seal the lid during the cooking.
6. Cook for about 4 hours in a slow oven (275°F)

TRIPE A LA FERMIERE

1 lb cooked tripe	butter (2 oz approx)
2 onions, peeled and diced	2 tbsp flour
½ lb diced carrots	seasoning
2 oz mushrooms	½ pint stock

1. Lightly brown chopped onion and diced carrots in butter.
2. Sprinkle with flour, allow to cool slightly.
3. Add stock, bring to boil for 3/4 minutes
4. Add cooked tripe and seasoning. Cover and cook for 1½ hours at a low temperature.
5. Slice and fry mushrooms in butter. Add to dish approx 10 minutes before end of cooking time.

TRIPE A LA BOURGEOISE

1-1½ lbs cooked tripe	parsley (chopped)
12 small onions	½ pint stock
1-2oz flour	bouquet garni
2 oz butter	1 lb new carrots
	(about 2 dozen small)

1. Lightly brown onions in butter. Sprinkle with flour and parsley, allow to brown a little.
2. Place tripe (previously cut into squares) into a saucepan, season.
3. Add bouquet garni. Bring to boil quickly.
4. Add new carrots and onions. Cover and simmer for 1½ hours.
5. Turn into a serving dish and garnish with parsley.

TRIPE AU GRATIN

1 lb tripe (cut into squares)	1 oz butter
1 oz flour	bouquet garni
½ pint milk	4 oz asparagus
2 oz grated cheese	1 each onion, carrot,
	diced

1. Make Bechamel sauce by usual method. Add tripe to sauce and cook on a low heat for about 10 minutes.
2. Place cooked asparagus in bottom of heat-proof dish. Place tripe mixture over it, and sprinkle with grated cheese.
3. Cook in a hot oven (400°F) until cheese is a golden brown.
4. Serve with hot, saute potatoes.

* * * * *

Greece

TRIPE SOUP
(Patsa)

2/3 lb tripe (cut into small pieces)
salt and pepper to season
2/3 cloves pounded garlic   rind of ½ lemon
egg and lemon sauce   onion, celery, etc, as
liked

1. Boil tripe in a stock of about 3 pints water, seasoning and lemon rind, for approx ½ hour.
2. Add other vegetables as required. Reduce heat and simmer until required.
3. Just before serving add egg and lemon sauce.

Egg & Lemon Sauce

4 egg yolks (or 2/3 whole eggs)
4 tablesp lemon juice
2/3 tablespoons taken from the stock

1. Beat the egg yolks until bubbly.
2. Slowly add the lemon juice, beating all the time.
3. Gradually add 2 or 3 tablespoons of the liquid from the dish being prepared.
4. Stir the sauce into the dish. Leave for 5 minutes on side of cooker, keeping the pan lid on. Do not allow the sauce to boil.

A SOUP FOR EASTER

1 lb lamb's tripe	1 bunch spring onions
4 lamb's trotters	parsley; dill
1 lamb's heart celery	2 oz rice
½ lb lamb's liver (chopped)	salt, pepper

1. Cook trotters and heart in a large saucepan of water, until a good stock is produced.
2. Remove from heat. Take out bones from trotters; slice up the heart; return both to the pan.
3. Add lamb's liver, chopped spring onions, chopped celery, parsley, dill, rice, salt and pepper.
4. Cook fairly rapidly until rice is soft. Remove from heat.
5. Add egg and lemon sauce. Simmer for 5-10 minutes over a low heat. This dish is sufficient for 6 to 8 people.

TRIPE SOUP
(Another variation: Souppa Skembes)

1 lb fresh tripe   1½ pints cold water
2 celery stalks, cut into thirds
1 onion, peeled and quartered
egg and lemon sauce   salt, pepper to taste

1. Cut tripe into 1" squares, boil up quickly in a pan of water, drain.
2. Cover with 1½ pints cold water. Add onion, celery and seasoning.
3. Bring to boil. Reduce heat and simmer until tripe is tender, adding more water if necessary.
4. Mix egg and lemon sauce into the soup gradually, over a low heat. Serve.

TRIPE STEW WITH HERBS
(Skembes Yahnistos)

2 lbs fresh tripe, cut into small squares	
¼ cup fresh thyme	1 chopped onion
1 bay leaf	¼ cup olive oil
1 cup chicken stock	1 clove garlic, mashed
salt, pepper	

1. Heat olive oil in a heavy casserole. Add onion to cook until browned.
2. Stir in fresh tripe. Cook over high heat for 5 minutes.
3. Add rest of ingredients, and enough water to cover. Bring to boil.
4. Reduce heat and simmer until tripe is tender, keeping lid on. The sauce should be quite thick when done. (Serves 6-8)

* * * * *

Hungary

TRIPE FRICASSEE
(Pacalbecsinalt)

1½lb tripe	vegetable stock
1 tablesp finely chopped parsley	2 oz lard
juice of 1 lemon	1 tablesp flour
⅓ pint sour cream	1 teaspoon salt

1. Cut tripe into 2" squares; cook in about 2 pints vegetable stock.
2. Lift out when tender and cut into thin strips

3. Heat the lard in a saucepan, add the flour and stir till frothy.
4. Add the chopped parsley, and pour over half the vegetable stock. Bring to boil.
5. Simmer for 2 minutes; add tripe and lemon juice.
6. Add sour cream and bring up to just boiling point. Serve in a deep bowl.

BREADED TRIPE CUTLETS
(Rantott pacal)

1½ lb tripe	1 teasp salt
1 egg	3 oz dried breadcrumbs
3 oz flour	fat to fry
tartare sauce	

1. Cut tripe into 2" squares, and cook in salted water until tender.
2. Drain. Dip tripe pieces first in flour, then beaten egg, then breadcrumbs.
3. Fry in deep fat. Serve with tartare sauce.

* * * * *

Italy

TRIPE SOUP
(from Piemonte)

3 tbsp olive oil	1 carrot	rosemary
1 cabbage (about ½ lb)	1 chopped onion
salt, pepper	stale bread
1 teasp butter	1 tablesp tomato sauce
7½ oz tripe cut in strips	2 oz lard
4 potatoes	parmesan cheese

1. Fry chopped onion, butter, lard, carrot and rosemary in the oil.
2. Sieve, and add to tripe cut into strips. Add salt and pepper to season.
3. Add stock sufficient for 4 people, and tomato sauce.
4. Boil for ¼ hour, add chopped potatoes and cabbage leaves. Soup is ready when potatoes are cooked.
5. Place a slice of stale bread on each plate and pour soup over. Sprinkle generously with parmesan cheese.

TRIPE IN SAUCE
(An ancient recipe of the "Confraternita d'la Tripa" of Moncalieri)

1¼ lb washed tripe, cut into thin strips
½ onion, thinly sliced   3 oz butter
2 oz lard   2 chopped cloves of garlic
100gms calf's foot, boned
salt, pepper, pinch of grated nutmeg
meat stock, parmesan cheese, grated
slices of toast, sufficient for 4 people

1. Fry onion slices in butter. When lightly browned, add the lard and garlic, still keeping on the heat.
2. Add the calf's foot, seasoning, nutmeg. Simmer until liquid almost used up.
3. Add the meat stock, simmer for 1/2 hours on a low heat.
4. Before serving sprinkle with parmesan cheese. Serve with slices of toast.

BEANS AND TRIPE SALAD
(Another recipe of the "Confraternita d'la Tripa")
10 oz cooked tripe, cut into short thin strips
3 oz cooked white Spanish beans
oil, lemon, salt, pepper, chopped parsley

1. Put all ingredients in salad bowl. Mix well together. Garnish with a few pieces of parsley.
2. Serve.

TRIPE CASSEROLE
2 lbs fresh cooked tripe (cut into thin strips)
I each of the following: small carrot, small onion, stalk celery, tablesp parsley (chopped).

½ cup each of the following: olive oil, chopped onion, chopped celery, chopped carrot, etc. (1 large can mixed vegetables would be a good substitute.)
2 cloves crushed garlic
¼ teasp chopped rosemary
⅔ cup dry white wine   1 cup canned tomatoes
2 teasp salt, pepper to taste
meat stock (about ½ pint)
grated Parmesan cheese

1. Boil up the carrot, onion and celery in a large pan of water. Add tripe and cook for several more minutes.
2. Pre-heat oven to 325°F. Meanwhile, if fresh chopped vegetables are used, cook on a medium heat for several minutes, adding garlic, parsley and rosemary. Continue to cook and stir for 2 to 3 more minutes.
3. Add tripe, and cook for 5 more minutes. Add white wine, tomato juice with tomatoes, seasoning and stock and bring up to boil once more.
4. Put into casserole dish and cook in oven for about 2 hours.
5. When cooked, remove lid and swirl in 2 tablespoons butter and grated cheese.
6. Serve very hot. (Serves 6)
NB: If liked, a 6 or 8 oz tin of butter beans may be added to the dish about 10 minutes before serving, for extra flavour.

* * * * *

Portugal

TRIPAS A PORTUGUESA

2¼ lbs tripe (calf's)	1 small calf's foot
2 oz chourico	3 oz streaky bacon
1 small fowl (jointed)	5 oz pickled pig's ear
1 small onion (about 1½ oz)	3½ oz carrots
½ oz lard	1 cup butter or haricot beans
sprig parsley	salt, pepper

(Note: chourico is smoked pork sausage, spiced with garlic and paprika; possibly black pudding would make an acceptable substitute.)

1. Cook the tripe, if not ready cooked, in about 2 pints of water with 2 teaspoons salt for about 3 hours.
2. Similarly half cook the calf's foot in a little water with some salt.
3. Heat the beans in water till boiling. Leave to stand for an hour.
4. Simmer separately the chicken, chopped sausage and bacon slices, covered with water, for about 30 minutes.
5. In a casserole put the lard, chopped onion and parsley; when onion is cooked but NOT brown, add the tripe, cut into pieces, the calf's foot, chicken, sausage, bacon, pig's ear, beans, raw carrots cut in rounds, salt and pepper.
6. Cook gently in broth from the meat until chicken, beans and carrots are tender (about an hour). The final consistency should be that of a stew. Serve with savoury rice.

Portuguese Savoury Rice
1. Put enough oil in a pan to cover the bottom.
2. Add a finely chopped, medium sized onion, cook over a low heat until lightly browned, stirring occasionally to prevent burning.
3. Mix in the dry rice until evenly coated.
4. Add boiling water (2 cups water to 1 cup rice) gradually, stirring all the time.
5. Cover pan, reduce heat, and allow to boil slowly for 20-30 minutes. The grains should look separated and not mushy.

DOBRADA A PORTUGUESA
(Tripe with haricot beans)
1 lb dried haricot beans   1 glass white wine
2 onions, finely chopped   1 tablespoon flour
4 tomatoes, peeled & chopped   a little water
½ pint stock, made from a cube   ½ lb chourico
2 chopped cloves garlic   7 oz chopped ham
4 oz belly of pork, minced   2 carrots, diced
2 lb tripe, cut into strips or squares
1 sprig thyme   ½ glass port   salt & pepper

1. Soak haricot beans overnight in plenty of water.
2. Bring beans and water to boil. Boil for 2-5 minutes, then simmer for 2½ hours or until beans are tender. Drain and put aside.
3. Fry chopped onion slowly with garlic, pork and chourico. (No fat is required, as the pork contains enough.)
4. After 10 minutes add the thyme and white wine. Continue to fry until the liquid is reduced by half.
5. Add the chopped tomatoes, stock, flour mixed with a little cold water, the chopped ham and diced carrots.
6. Leave to cook for a few more minutes, then transfer to a stewpot and add the tripe and haricot beans. Season and add the port last of all.
7. Cook slowly for a further half hour before serving.

* * * * *

Spain

TRIPE MADRID STYLE
(Callos a la Madrilena)
2 lb ready cooked tripe, cut into strips
3½ oz chorizo (garlic sausage)
1 pig's foot, cooked and boned
20 gms tomato puree   2 chillis, chopped fine
2 tbsp olive oil   1 chopped onion
4 oz cooked ham, minced   2 tbsp flour
salt, pepper; chopped parsley

1. Put tripe and pig's foot in a stewpan, over a low heat.
2. Meanwhile fry the chopped onion for about 10 minutes, then add ham, chorizo and tomato puree. Continue cooking for a further few minutes.
3. Add flour mixed with a little of the broth from the tripe, stir well.
4. Pour mixture into the stewpan. Add chillies and salt and pepper.
5. Cook very slowly for 15 minutes.
6. Sprinkle with parsley just before serving. Serve very hot.

* * * * *

Turkey

KHASH or PACA
(Tripe and trotter stew)
4 trotters or calf's feet, boned   1 oz butter
6 lambs' tongues, cut up   ½ teaspoon paprika
2 lb calf's tripe   3 cloves garlic, crushed
1 tablespoon chopped fresh mint
1 tablespoon chopped fresh parsley
salt & pepper to taste   juice of 1 lemon

1. Put tripe, trotters and tongues into a pan, with enough water to cover.
2. Season, cook over a low heat for ½ hour.
3. Melt butter in a small saucepan, add garlic and paprika, saute for a few minutes, stirring frequently. Stir in the mint and parsley.

4. Add to the meat stew. Continue cooking until meat is tender.
5. Serve in soup bowls. Sprinkle over lemon juice before eating.

* * * * *

The Middle East

ISKEMBE
1 lb sheep's tripe   1 lemon
½ pint milk   3-4 cloves garlic
1 large onion, sliced   salt, pepper
1 oz flour   1 oz butter   ½ pint water
3 sprigs parsley, finely chopped

1. Put tripe in a pan, cover with milk, water, sliced onion and salt. Simmer for about half an hour.
2. Take tripe out, cut into thin strips and lay them on a serving dish.
3. Make a roux with the butter and flour, add tripe milk, then lemon juice, crushed garlic, chopped parsley and seasoning.
4. Bring the sauce up to boil until thickened, then pour over tripe and serve immediately.

NOHUTLU ISKEMBE
(Tripe with chick peas)
1 lb sheep's tripe, cooked and cut into small squares
1 lemon   ½ lb chick peas
salt   4 oz butter
2 medium onions   3 cloves garlic
black pepper   water

1. Soak chick peas overnight. Put into fresh water, boil for about an hour, or until soft.
2. Simmer tripe in water (enough to cover) with two strips of lemon rind, crushed garlic and salt, for about half an hour.
3. Fry sliced onion in butter until clear, and stir in the drained peas.
4. Add black pepper, salt and tripe, with about a pint of the tripe liquid (discard the lemon rind).
5. Simmer for a further 20 minutes. Serve hot; a good accompaniment would be a lemon sauce or paprika and chillies.

PACA HASLAMASI
(Stewed sheep's trotters)
4 sheep's trotters   1 lemon
1 tbs finely chopped parsley   1 tbs vinegar
3 cloves garlic   salt
1 tbs olive oil

1. Cover trotters with water, lemon rind, 1 clove of garlic (crushed), olive oil and salt.
2. Simmer for 3-4 hours, skimming off scum if necessary.
3. When cooked through, remove meat and place on a serving dish with a little of the broth.
4. Serve with a sauce made from vinegar, 2 crushed garlic cloves and parsley all mixed together; alternatively, plain yoghurt with a sprinkling of paprika over.
NB: Trotters need long, slow cooking, preferably overnight.

* * * * *

Africa

TRIPE STEW
1 lb cooked tripe, cut into one inch squares
½ lb cooked spinach (fresh or canned)
½ lb diced onion   ½ tsp nutmeg (optional)